T0208430

HONORING
GOD
WITH YOUR
MONEY

Susan E. Ball

WESTBOW
PRESS®
A DIVISION OF THOMAS NELSON
& ZONDERVAN

WestBow Press books may be ordered through booksellers or by contacting:

WestBow Press
A Division of Thomas Nelson & Zondervan
1663 Liberty Drive
Bloomington, IN 47403
www.westbowpress.com
844-714-3454

ISBN: 978-1-6642-1826-0 (sc)
ISBN: 978-1-6642-1825-3 (hc)
ISBN: 978-1-6642-1827-7 (e)

Library of Congress Control Number: 2021902120

Print information available on the last page.

WestBow Press rev. date: 02/02/2021

PREFACE

The seed for this book grew out of a personal Bible study I completed in early 2013. After reading *Pleasure and Profit in Bible Study* by Dwight L. Moody, I felt challenged to study God's Word in a new way. I had read through the Bible many times, and I had completed numerous Bible studies using someone else's materials. I knew it was time to complete a study on my own. I started by picking a topic and thoroughly seeking out what the Bible had to say on that chosen topic. Having a background in mathematics and finance, it seemed natural to land on the subject of money.

I started by reading each verse that contained the word "money" and other related words, including "treasure" and "riches." The Bible has many verses that address wealth, income, riches, poverty, giving, and treasure. The idea came to my mind that the materials I was gathering should be shared with others. This motivated me to develop a series of lessons for a Sunday School class and to post the lessons on my blog. The culmination of all the word studies, Bible verses, and lessons is brought together in this book.

I believe that Christians should strive to honor God in every aspect of their lives. Money is one area that seems to give many people difficulty. My prayer is that this Bible study will help each reader to have a clearer understanding of how to manage and to use the financial resources God entrusts to them in such a way as to provide for their families and to bring honor and glory to God.

ACKNOWLEDGMENTS

First of all, I want to acknowledge my parents for instilling in me sound money management principles. They taught these principles through their regular habits of tithing and giving offerings to the church, supporting missions and charitable organizations, paying their bills promptly, using debt sparingly, and helping me to establish credit when I reached adulthood. These principles have served me well over my lifetime.

After receiving my MBA from the University of Florida, I worked for Dr. Eugene Brigham, the leading finance textbook author in the world at that time. As I learned about the world of book publishing, I was privileged to co-author two books on financial management with Dr. Brigham.

Arnold Lastinger, my pastor at First Assembly of God in Gainesville, FL, taught biblical money management concepts to our congregation and worked with church members to create their family budgets. I was honored to assist him in this endeavor and ever since have helped people develop their budgets. Pastor Lastinger faithfully lived out the principles he taught and served as an excellent role model. His teachings introduced me to the budgeting and money management materials developed by Larry Burkett and Crown Financial Ministries.

Stacey Whitman has encouraged me and assisted me in getting this material ready for publication. She provided editorial guidance, and the book is much better for her keen insights. Stacey also suggested that I create additional materials to enhance this study and to accompany this book that could be used by Sunday school teachers and small group leaders. Teaching materials have been developed and are available to those who want them by emailing me at susan.ball5@aol.com.

And most importantly, I want to acknowledge the love and support of my husband, Steve. What a joy it is to share my life with him. His encouragement and belief in me allow me to excel in all the work that the Lord calls me to do. And, of course, I am eternally grateful to my Lord and Savior Jesus Christ. His precious gift of salvation assures me of a home in Heaven and an incredible journey on Earth as I strive to fulfill the plan He has for my life.

CONTENTS

INTRODUCTION

In January 2009, my family experienced first-hand the effects of the Great Recession. Following the Christmas and New Year's holidays, my husband, Steve, received notice at work that he was being laid off immediately. Steve's earnings comprised 70 percent of our combined income. Rather than allowing fear to take over our feelings, we experienced "the peace of God, which surpasses all understanding." (Philippians 4:7). We had walked with the Lord for many years, and we had learned to trust God in all our circumstances. We firmly believed that God would see us through this challenge because we had practiced tithing and managed our money according to Biblical principles. Even though Steve's period of unemployment would last for nearly three years, we could immediately see how God had prepared us for this season in our lives. God was true to His promises. He provided for our every need, and we continued to honor Him with our money. Throughout the book, I will share more about this story of trusting in the Lord during hard financial times.

By profession, I am a small business consultant. I specialize in helping people establish and grow small businesses. It is exciting to be a small part of helping a prospective business owner fulfill his or her entrepreneurial dreams of creating a successful business. Success is only possible when the person has prepared by saving money to invest in the business, maintaining a good credit rating, and limiting their use of debt. On too many occasions, I meet with someone who has a good idea, plus the ability and the passion for running a business, yet poor credit or a lack of financial resources thwart their plans. Without his own money to invest in his business and without a good credit score, the prospective business owner cannot borrow the funds needed to start a business.

I believe that the root of financial problems is our failure to fully understand how we should use the money that God entrusts to us. The Bible instructs us on the role money should play in our lives. We can apply the Biblical principles, written so long ago, as a guideline for how to live in financial freedom. If we follow God's instructions and use our financial resources in ways that bring honor to God, then we will find that we can live well within our means. Our stress levels will go down, and we will be more content with our lives. Additionally, God promises to financially and spiritually bless those who honor Him by using their money to support the church's work and assist those in need. The purpose of this Bible study is to acquaint the reader with the Biblical principles of money management presented in God's Word and to help him or her to put those principles into practice.

If you are participating in this Bible study, but you do not know Jesus Christ as your Lord and Savior, I urge you to take steps to correct that immediately. Having a personal relationship with the Lord will open a new door to your understanding of these financial guidelines. You can find information on God's plan of salvation in Appendix B at the end of this book.

HOW TO USE THIS STUDY

In the first part of the study, we will investigate what the Bible says about money and how we should use it. The second part of the Bible study examines money management principles and teaches practical methods of applying those principles to establish and maintain budgets.

To get the most out of this study, you should:

1) Record all of your income and expenses for at least a month.
2) Begin journaling the ways God blesses you financially during this study.
3) Use the space provided to write your thoughts and answers to questions.
4) Pray daily, asking God to help you to honor Him through how you spend your money.

Unless otherwise specified, all Scriptures are quoted from the New King James Version (NKJV), 1982, Thomas Nelson. New International Version (NIV) references are from the 1984 version, by Biblica, Inc. New American Standard (NAS) references are from various editions put out by The Lockman Foundation. Scriptures are quoted as referenced on BibleHub.com. References from The Message are from *The Message: The Bible in Contemporary Language*, by Eugene Peterson, 2002, Navpress.

The Purpose of Money

Billy Graham said, "If a person gets his attitude toward money straight, it will help straighten out almost every other area in his life." This is a powerful reminder that should inspire all of us to work diligently to accomplish the goal of cultivating a proper attitude toward money. My prayer is that as you work through the lessons in this book, God will help you develop the right attitude toward money—one that will lead you to honor God with your money and with every aspect of your life.

Before we can consider how to develop a proper attitude and honor God with our money, we need to consider the purpose of money.

Think About: What purposes does money serve?

_____

_____

_____

Think About: Without money, or another medium of exchange, how would you acquire food, clothing, and other necessities?

_____

_____

_____

Merriam-Webster.com defines money as "something generally accepted as a medium of exchange, a measure of value, or a means of payment."

Money plays an essential role in our lives. We all need to acquire food, shelter, clothing, and other necessities. Money serves to make transactions easier. Without money, we would have to barter for the things we need and want. Work is a form of barter. I go to work for you and give up my free time. While I am at work, I accomplish the tasks you assign to me. In exchange for my time and labor, you pay me an agreed-upon sum. Without money, I would have to trade my services to you for products or services that I need and that you would supply. If you did not have the goods that I was willing to work for, you would have to trade with others to get them, or I would have to work for someone who did have them. Bartering systems are inefficient and time-consuming. Money makes the whole process much more straightforward.

Most of us work hard to earn our money, and we want to get the most for it. We use the money we make to meet our needs and to make life easier and more enjoyable.

Read Isaiah 55:2. It provides a useful framework for money management.

"Why do you spend money for what is not bread, And your wages for what does not satisfy?"

➤ In this verse, what does bread signify?

_____

_____

_____

➤ When have you spent your money on things that brought no satisfaction?

_____

_____

_____

Bread signifies necessities of life--food, shelter, clothing, and other things we genuinely need. If we spend our money to buy the things we need, we feel satisfied and contented. When we waste our money on something that we do not need, we feel regret and discontentment. All of us have purchased things we _thought_ we really wanted, only to have them sit in a closet unused for months or years before we decided to get rid of them. At the time of the purchase, we felt a sense of satisfaction or a bit of a thrill at having found the perfect purse, shoes, sweater, couch, exercise machine, or whatever it is we had just bought. However, that feeling did not last long if the product was something we did not genuinely need. Our natural tendency to purchase items we do not need has led to the rise of yard sales and thrift stores.

Retailers count on us buying things that are not essential. Advertisers create ads to spark an appetite for "need" within us. As a business consultant, I encourage my clients to frame their marketing efforts to show how their products or services will satisfy their customers' needs and turn wants into needs. Their job is to try to sell their products and services. As a consumer, you should determine if you need the item offered and make a buying decision that meets your needs and fits within your budget.

We would waste much less money if, before we make a purchase, we would stop and ask ourselves two questions:

1) Do I truly need this item?
2) Am I willing to trade _____ hour(s) of my labor to obtain this item?

As you go through this Bible study, I encourage you to pause before making any discretionary purchases and consider those questions. If you remember to ask yourself those questions, you should find yourself purchasing fewer items and being happier with those you buy.

Rainbow Vacuum Cleaner: In the mid-1980s, an acquaintance came to our home and demonstrated an incredible product, the Rainbow Vacuum Cleaner. The vacuum suctioned up dirt into a canister of water and provided visible evidence of how much dirt was trapped in the carpet. It seemed like a great product; however, the price tag was quite hefty—about $1,000, which is the equivalent of $2,850 today. We wanted the vacuum, but we were hesitant to spend that much money. The salesman warned us that the price was only good for that evening. If we took even one day to think about it, the price would go up significantly. We succumbed to the pressure and bought the vacuum cleaner. It was not long before we discovered how unpleasant it was to dump out the dirty water and clean the canister. Moreover, we were not truly convinced that it cleaned better than our other vacuum cleaner. We came to resent the purchase.

Fortunately, God had mercy on us. Steve's co-worker mentioned that she really wanted a Rainbow Vacuum Cleaner and regretted not buying one when she was given a demonstration. Steve sold her our vacuum cleaner for $500, and both parties were happy.

Steve and I learned not to yield to pressure to buy an item on the spot. Since that time, if a salesperson tells us that we must purchase today or that the price will be higher later, one of us will say, "Remember the Rainbow Vacuum," and we walk away. This principle has served us well and helped us avoid future mistakes.

Activity: Make a list of some purchases you have regretted.

_____

_____

_____

_____

_____

_____

Why did you regret spending your money on these items?

_____

_____

If you could have back the money you spent on those items, what would the money allow you to do?

_____

_____

Lesson from the Teachings of Christ: The Parable of the Prodigal Son

Jesus told the parable of the prodigal son in the book of Luke. Teachers often use this parable to illustrate God's amazing love and grace towards His children. However, it is a story that can teach us some critical financial principles. A synopsis of the story is below, and you can read the complete story in Luke 15:11 – 32.

The story begins with, _"A certain man had two sons. And the younger of them said to his father, 'Father, give me the portion of the goods that falls to me.' So he divided to them his livelihood."_

The younger son left home and engaged in wild living. He blew through his inheritance quickly. About the time he ran out of money, a severe famine struck the country. The younger son found himself without friends and in need of a job. The only job he was able to get was feeding pigs.

Eventually, the younger son became so desperate that he decided to return home and throw himself on his father's mercy. The father rejoiced to have his errant son home and threw a feast to celebrate. The older brother became angry and refused to join in the celebration. His father explained that he had to celebrate the younger son's return and that the older son was entitled to anything that belongs to the father. All he had to do was ask.

Think About: What does this parable teach us about money?

_____

_____

_____

_____

From a financial point of view, this story illustrates the following principles:

1) Money was not the answer to the prodigal son's problems, and it is never the solution to our problems. The son thought that having money and the freedom to spend it as he chose would make him happy. He learned that the money did not bring him lasting happiness. In fact, it led him into bondage. Money is necessary in our society to buy the things we need, but money will never make us a better person or bring lasting happiness.

2) Sometimes, God gives us what we demand, even when it is not in our best interest. I do not imagine the father and son's conversation to be a peaceful or cordial dialogue in the story. Instead, I envision a son pestering his dad for weeks or months to give him his share. Although the father does not think it is in his son's best interest, he eventually gives in to his son's demands. We like to believe that

God gives us only what is good for us; however, the Bible clearly states that sometimes God gives us what we demand, even though He knows it is not what is best for us. An example of this is when God gave in to Israel's desire for a king. God warned the Israelites that a king would oppress and tax them, yet they were undeterred in their demands (1 Samuel 8). God yielded to their demands and allowed them to learn for themselves that God's plans are the best plans.

3) Wealth that is not earned is not appreciated. The younger son did not value his father's money because he did not work for it. It did not cost him many hours of labor, so he thought little of wasting it on frivolities. He did not appreciate what he had until he had lost it all.

4) You cannot buy real friends. As the prodigal son learned, fair-weather friends will scatter when the money is gone. Unfortunately, many celebrities have had to learn this lesson the hard way. They are surrounded by so-called friends when they are at the height of their careers. When their careers begin to wane, and the money no longer flows freely, many of those false friends scatter and look for another rising star to befriend.

5) All that the Father has He shares with His children. If you are a child of God, all the riches of Heaven are available to you. The availability of riches does not mean that God is going to give them to you (reread point 2). However, it does mean that you should make your needs known to God and ask Him to meet them. God promises to take care of His children, and God always keeps His promises.

I hope that you will take the lessons of the prodigal son to heart. God desires His best for you. Often we want things that are not actually in our best interest. Trust God and allow Him to give you those things that will help you grow and mature in Him, and trust God when He withholds those things that will lead you away.

Think About: Have you ever strongly desired something and obtained it, only to find out that it did not live up to your expectations?

_____

_____

_____

True Wealth

Read Proverbs 22:1

"A good name is more desirable than great riches; to be esteemed is better than silver or gold." (NIV)

➢ According to this verse, what is the measure of true wealth?

_____

_____

➢ How is true wealth to be obtained?

_____

_____

Honoring God With Our Money

In the next several lessons of this Bible study, we will consider how we can honor God with our finances. Honoring God with money involves:

- earning money honestly
- spending money wisely
- giving back to the work of the Lord a portion of our earnings
- sharing with those less fortunate than ourselves

Accomplishing all four of these goals requires that we understand how God views money and have a plan for managing our money.

Life Application:

Proverbs 30:8 – 9 says, *"Remove falsehood and lies far from me, Give me neither poverty nor riches—Feed me with the food allotted to me; Lest I be full and deny You, And say, 'Who is the Lord?' Or lest I be poor and steal, And profane the name of my God."*

It is crucial to have a proper perspective on money. If money takes on a more important role than it should, we begin to desire money above all else. This desire can lead people to engage in foolish and illegal actions to obtain more money. To the extreme, many murderers, thieves, and embezzlers have been motivated by greed and the desire for wealth. Failure to place a proper value on money will lead to poor money management and the inability to meet our family's needs.

Solomon provides us with a proper perspective on how much money we genuinely need in the verses above. We should desire to have enough money to meet our family's needs and assist those less fortunate than us, without feeling pressured to engage in illegal activities. We never should desire to have so much money that we feel independent and self-sufficient. Proverbs 30:8 reminds us that God wants us to recognize that He is our provider. He gives us talents and the ability to work and earn money. We need to acknowledge His help and His gracious provision for us.

Think About: How has God provided for your needs this week? How have you seen His provision for you in the past?

_____

_____

_____

_____

LESSON 2

Warnings to the Rich

Occasionally I find myself daydreaming about what I would do if I suddenly acquired a great deal of wealth. I imagine that a long-lost relative left me a large sum of money, say $1 million, and I calculate how I would use it:

1) With whom I would share it and how much I would share
2) What charities I would support
3) How much I would set aside to allow me to feel secure in my retirement years

It's a common fantasy, and it's likely one you have indulged in, also. Your scenario may have been a bit different from mine. Perhaps you imagined your wealth would come through an inheritance, a lawsuit, or winnings from a game show or contest. The sum of money you dream about receiving may have increased over the years, as you realized that $1 million doesn't buy today what it did when you were a child.

Activity: Imagine for a moment that you have received $1 million. What will you do with the money?

_____

_____

_____

_____

The most common answers include: buy a house, pay off debt, save for the kids' college funds, and help family members. I hope your list includes giving back to God through tithing and helping others who have been less fortunate than you.

Think About: Would $1 million put you in a position never to work again? Would you want to be in such a situation?

_____

_____

_____

Think About: Would you do anything differently if your winnings were $10 million? How might such a large sum of money change your life?

_____

_____

_____

Think About: Would you want to have enough money to be able to retire at 40? 50?

_____

_____

_____

Ponder: As you read the scriptures in this lesson, you should consider the following questions:

- Does God want Christians to be wealthy?
- Does it seem that those raised in wealth have difficulty finding their place in life and frequently wind up bored and in trouble?
- Does wealth equate to happiness?

Read 1 Timothy 6:10.

"For the love of money is a root of all kinds of evil, for which some have strayed from the faith in their greediness, and pierced themselves through with many sorrows."

➤ What does this verse tell us is the root of all evil?

_____

➤ Why is the love of money a problem for many believers?

_____

_____

Money is not the root of all evil, but the love of money is "a root of all kinds of evil." Money in and of itself is not a problem. We all need money, and it is not wrong to want enough money to meet our needs and care for those around us. Problems arise when we love money. It has ruined many lives, and many crimes have been committed over money.

The love of money can be a problem for believers because having an excess amount of money leads to a spirit of self-sufficiency. The Bible clarifies that God wants believers to recognize their need for God and be dependent on Him. When we have more than enough money to meet our needs, we may not feel our need for God so deeply.

Read Ecclesiastes 5:10

"He who loves money will not be satisfied with money, nor he who loves abundance with its income." (NAS)

> ➤ According to this verse, the love of money leads to what?

_____

_____

The love of money leads to a spirit of discontentment. Wealthy people often hoard money, well above the amount they need for retirement. Rather than using their money to care for others and share God's love, they become anxious to have a larger and larger bank account.

I have been a Christian for more than 50 years. God has proven the truth of His word to me many times. I don't need scholarly or scientific studies to verify to me that God's Word is true. Yet, many people do, so I am always excited when "worldly" studies draw conclusions that support God's word.

A survey of 165 super-rich households confirmed the truth of Ecclesiastes 5:10. The respondents in this survey had an average net worth of $78 million, yet most expressed Solomon's same sentiments: they did not feel they had enough wealth and did not feel financially secure.

Fears of the Super-Rich

Despite having an abundance of wealth that most of us cannot imagine, the super-wealthy are generally plagued with anxieties about love, work, and family and do not feel financially secure. Graeme Wood drew these conclusions in an article entitled "Secret Fears of the Super-Rich." The Atlantic Magazine published the piece in 2011.[1]

Mr. Wood reviewed the findings, and his conclusions show that not only does money not buy happiness but that at some point, an overabundance of money becomes a burden.

Here are some of the conclusions Mr. Wood drew from the survey:

1) People don't know how to deal with an excessive amount of money. Even when they had so much money that it became burdensome, they still desired to have more.
2) Constant luxury is, in a sense, no luxury at all.
3) Being extremely wealthy is no more fulfilling than merely being prosperous.
4) The very wealthy believe they have lost their right to complain because they fear others will find them ungrateful.
5) The very wealthy worry about their children: Will the money spoil them? Will they lead meaningful lives? Will someone love them for themselves and not just their money?
6) Money interferes with their relationships. They wonder if people like them just for their money, and they feel they must always "treat" others. They rarely get to experience having someone else pick up the check.
7) Extreme wealth takes away some of the real joys of living, such as holidays—people expect the wealthy to give extravagant gifts; gifts received are not so meaningful when you can buy whatever you want.
8) Those who inherited their wealth question their self-worth.
9) The wealthy have a difficult time with work. Society may view those who do work in our present economy as having taken a

job someone else needs. Also, it is easy for the wealthy to quit a position as soon as a situation arises that they don't like.

10) The happiest wealthy people are usually heavily involved in philanthropy.

Many of these conclusions mirror truths found in God's word. For example, the respondents felt they would be secure if they only had 25 percent more money. That sounds a lot like what God's word teaches us in Ecclesiastes 5:10, *"He who loves money will not be satisfied with money."*

God's word also teaches us that *"It is more blessed to give than to receive."* (Acts 20:35) Those super-wealthy individuals who engage in philanthropy have learned this for themselves.

While we may dream of becoming super-wealthy one day, we need to realize that having excess money above what we genuinely need will not make us happy. Happiness and true contentment can only be found in Jesus Christ.

Lesson from the Teachings of Christ: The Rich Young Ruler

The story of the Rich Young Ruler is told in Matthew 19:16 – 30. Jesus used this story to demonstrate how difficult it is for those who love money to be saved. To recap, the young ruler asked Jesus what he had to do to earn eternal life. Jesus replied that he should keep God's commandments. He responded that he had kept the commandments and asked what he lacked. Jesus then told him to sell all that he had and give the money to the poor and then follow Jesus. In verse 22, we read, *"When the young man heard this, he went away sorrowful, for he had great possessions."*

Then Jesus told his disciples, *"Assuredly, I say to you that it is hard for a rich man to enter the kingdom of heaven. And again I say to you, it is easier for a camel to go through the eye of a needle than for a rich man to enter the kingdom of God."* (Matthew 19:23 – 24)

➤ Why do you think it is so hard for the rich to be saved?

_____

_____

_____

➤ Why was the rich ruler sad?

_____

_____

_____

➤ Obviously, it is impossible for a camel to go through the eye of a needle. Yet, Christ taught that it was easier for that to happen than for a rich man to be saved. Was Jesus declaring that the rich cannot be saved?

_____

_____

_____

People often come to God when they face a need in their lives that they cannot meet. The need might be spiritual, emotional, physical, or financial. Rich people have a more challenging time realizing their need for God because their riches increase their feelings of self-sufficiency. They may also love their fortunes, as the rich young ruler did in this parable. He was sad because he realized his need for salvation, yet he wasn't willing to give up earthly treasure for true riches in Heaven.

Of course, many wealthy people are saved. In Matthew 19:23 – 24, Jesus was saying that it is harder for the rich to be saved than for the poor. It is so hard that on their own, it would be impossible. Yet, with God, all things are possible—a camel can go through the eye of a needle, or a rich man can see his need for salvation. We should keep in mind that none of us come to God on our own. God has to draw us and open our hearts and our minds to receive His word.

Additional Warnings to the Rich

The Bible provides many additional warnings to the rich. Look up the following verses in the NKJV and fill-in the missing words. As you do, allow God to reveal to you the dangers of seeking riches for the sake of being rich.

1 Timothy 6:9 But those who desire to be rich fall into _____ and a snare, and into many foolish and _____ lusts which drown men in destruction and _____.

Job 36:19 Will your _____, or all the mighty forces, keep you from_____?

Luke 6:24 But woe to you who are _____, for you have received your _____.

Luke 1:53 He has filled the _____ with good things, and the rich He has sent away _____.

James 5:1 – 5 Come now, you _____, weep and howl for your _____ that are coming upon you. Your riches are _____, and your _____ are moth eaten. Your gold and silver are _____...You have heaped up _____in the last days...You have lived on earth in _____ and luxury.

➢ After reading these verses and considering the study on the fears of the super-rich, why might you still desire to be rich?

_____

_____

_____

_____

Many of us desire a level of riches that will allow us to be debt-free and experience financial freedom. Wealth also gives us the ability to help others. Being rich is not a sin, but loving money above others is a sin.

Life Application:

In Hebrews 13:5, we read, *"Keep your lives free from the love of money and be content with what you have, because God has said, 'Never will I leave you; never will I forsake you.'"* (NIV)

We need to learn to be content with what God chooses to give us. He knows what is best for us and what will allow us to honor Him. We need to be satisfied and live within our means, regardless of the level of income God provides for our family and us. We need to trust that He will provide for all our needs.

If you are struggling to be content in your current circumstance, strive to become more thankful by focusing on what you do have instead of what you lack. Make a conscious effort to thank God throughout each day for the many blessings in your life. For example: on laundry day, rather than focusing on the piles of dirty clothes, thank God that you have a family who needs you to care for their clothing and thank Him for your washing machine. As you wash dishes, thank God for hot and cold running water and that you have access to safe, clean water. These are blessings that people in many countries do not enjoy. Philippians 4:8 instructs us to direct our focus on the things of God. *"Finally, brethren, whatever things are true, whatever things are noble, whatever things are just, whatever things are pure, whatever things are lovely, whatever things are of good report, if there is any virtue and if there is anything praiseworthy-meditate on these things."* If you follow this mandate, you will cultivate a spirit of thankfulness and contentment.

This week try to focus on being content. Ask God to help you be content with what you have and trust Him to meet your needs. As God leads you, pray the prayer below and record some of the ways you have noticed yourself becoming more content.

_____

_____

_____

_____

Prayer:

Heavenly Father,

Thank You for loving me and calling me to be Your child. I acknowledge that Your ways are higher than my ways and that Your plans for my life are infinitely better than the plans I could come up with on my own. I ask that You create within me a spirit of contentment. Help me be satisfied with the wealth that You, Lord, provide me and use that wealth to care for my family and share with others. May I always honor and glorify You in the way I handle the money You have entrusted to me. In the name of Jesus, I ask this. Amen.

Note:

[1]"Secret Fears of the Super-Rich," by Graeme Wood, published in *The Atlantic* Magazine, April 2011.

LESSON 3

Frivolity of Trusting in Wealth

Many people put more faith in their bank balances than in God to provide for their needs. The economic crisis of 2007 – 2009 proved God's word to be correct when it instructs us not to trust in wealth. The average American saw 40 percent of their wealth evaporate when the stock market crashed and home values plummeted. My family experienced a double blow when the crash hit our stock portfolio, and Steve lost his job. It was a challenging time, but our faith was firm, and we were confident that God would provide for all our needs. Trusting in God does not mean that we should not set aside money for retirement; it does mean that we should not let variabilities in the economy and the ups-and-downs of the stock market rattle us.

In this lesson, we will consider what the Bible says about wealth and poverty. As you work through it, think about the following questions:

1) Why are some Christians financially comfortable while others struggle financially?
2) Are wealthy Christians more "spiritual" than poorer Christians?

➤ Is there a connection between your spiritual condition and your bank balance?

What does the Bible tell us about wealth and poverty in the following verses?

➤ **1 Samuel 2:7** *"The Lord makes poor and rich; He brings low, He also exalts."* (NAS)

_____

_____

_____

➤ **James 1:9 – 11** *"Let the lowly brother glory in his exaltation, but the rich in his humiliation, because as a flower of the field he will pass away. For no sooner has the sun arisen with a burning heat than it withers the grass; its flower falls, and its beautiful appearance perishes. So the rich man also will fade away in his pursuits."*

_____

_____

_____

➤ **Psalm 49:16 – 17** *"Do not be afraid when one becomes rich, when the glory of his house is increased; for when he dies he shall carry nothing away; his glory shall not descend after him."*

_____

_____

_____

➢ **Proverbs 28:6** *"Better is the poor who walks in his integrity than one perverse in his ways, though he be rich."*

_____

_____

_____

These verses teach us that:

- God determines who is wealthy and who is poor. While we can take steps that affect our level of wealth, it is God who gives us the ability to earn wealth, and God can take it away in an instant. God also decides into which family and nation we are born. I do not know why I was blessed to be born into an American family that could support and care for me. I appreciate that God chose to bless me, and I realize that I need to share my blessings with those who are less fortunate.

- There is no shame in being poor. In America, we tend to assign worth based on bank account balances. The poor are often not accorded the same respect as their wealthier neighbors. However, Job 34: 18 – 19 tells us that God does not show partiality based on wealth. *"Is he not the One who says to kings, 'You are worthless,' and to nobles, 'You are wicked,' who shows no partiality to princes and does not favor the rich over the poor, for they are all the work of his hands?"*

- There is no glory in being rich. We tend to fawn all over celebrities and try to make acquaintances with those having wealth or power. However, God does not place a higher value on the wealthy than the poor, as we saw in the scripture above. If God blesses us with wealth, it is because God chose to bless us in that manner. We need to be very careful to credit God with our wealth and to use it in ways that honor Him. If we do not honor God with the wealth given to us, God may decide to transfer our wealth to someone who will use it for His purposes.

- It is tempting to think that more prosperous Christians are "more" spiritual than poorer Christians. However, an examination of

God's Word shows that wealth, or lack thereof, is no indication of one's spiritual condition. It may be a matter of trust, however. God does impart wealth to those who can be trusted to use it according to His purposes, and He withholds wealth from Christians for whom wealth would create problems.

- Righteousness is more desirable than riches. We place a high value on a large bank account, as it affords us the ability to meet our families' needs and indulge in luxuries. However, God's word clearly teaches us that wealth is not a measure of righteousness. You cannot use wealth to purchase your way into Heaven and eternal life. Right standing with God rewards us with eternal life. Of course, you can only be righteous through the blood of Jesus. We cannot earn righteousness; we can only accept Jesus's free gift of salvation and then strive to live a righteous life with God's help.

There are many people in the Bible whose lives illustrate these truths.

➢ As an example of incredible generosity, Jesus pointed out the poor widow who put her last few cents into the offering. Jesus looked at her heart and not the amount of her offering. (Mark 12: 41 – 44)

➢ Jesus told the story of the beggar Lazarus to his disciples to illustrate that wealth does not equate to righteousness. At the gate to his house, the rich man ignored the sick beggar. When they both died, Lazarus was received into Heaven while the rich man was tormented in hell. (Luke 16: 19 – 31)

➢ The Old Testament book of Job tells a powerful story about a man who suffered great financial and personal loss. God allowed Job's wealth, health, and children to be taken away from him. The loss was not due to his lack of faith or righteousness. Job was going through a time of testing. When the testing was over, God restored in a double portion all that Job had lost.

➢ God used John the Baptist to announce the coming of the Messiah. However, John lived a life of poverty and self-denial. In Matthew 3:4, we read that he "was clothed in camel's hair, with a leather belt around his waist; and his food was locusts and wild honey."

Role of the Wealthy

Read 1 Timothy 6:17 – 19

"Command those who are rich in this present age not to be haughty, nor to trust in uncertain riches but in the living God, who gives us richly all things to enjoy. Let them do good, that they be rich in good works, ready to give, willing to share, storing up for themselves a good foundation for the time to come, that they may lay hold on eternal life."

➢ What is the role of the wealthy in society?

_____

_____

This verse tells us that the wealthy's role is to do good deeds and be generous and bless others. If the rich use their money as God commanded, they will build treasure in Heaven. Our goal should be to build up eternal treasure, which will last forever. Earthly riches are fleeting and will not do us any good in Heaven.

Wealth should never go to our heads. We should never think more highly of ourselves because we have an above-average salary or because we have a considerable net worth. God does not give us wealth because we deserve it.

If God has blessed you with financial resources beyond what you need to provide for your family, please remember His command to share with those less fortunate than yourself. Pray and ask God to direct your giving to the needs He would have you meet. In this way, you will be a blessing, and you will store up treasure in Heaven.

Blessings Promised to the Poor

Read James 2:5 – 6

"Listen, my beloved brethren: Has God not chosen the poor of this world to be rich in faith and heirs of the kingdom which He promised to those who love Him? But you have dishonored the poor man. Do not the rich oppress you and drag you into the courts?"

> ➤ What blessings does God promise the poor?

_____

_____

This verse reminds us that God has promised blessings to the poor. If they love Him, they will be rich in faith and will inherit the kingdom of God. Those are pretty powerful blessings. The poor may not have as many creature comforts on Earth, but those who love the Lord have a glorious eternity in Heaven awaiting them. The same verse paraphrased in *The Message* puts it this way, *"He chose the world's down-and-out as the kingdom's first citizens, with full rights and privileges. This kingdom is promised to anyone who loves God."* In other words, the poor will not be considered second-class when they get to Heaven. They will be full-fledged sons and daughters of the King with all the rights and privileges of a King's child.

If your family is struggling financially, please remember that there is no shame in being poor and no shame in asking for help. Ask God to meet your needs, and then allow Him to do so by sharing your needs with others.

Lesson from the Teachings of Christ: The Parable of the Rich Fool (Luke 12:13 – 21)

> *Then one from the crowd said to Him, "Teacher, tell my brother to divide the inheritance with me."*

But He said to him, "Man, who made Me a judge or an arbiter over you?" And He said to them, "Take heed and beware of covetousness, for one's life does not consist in an abundance of the things he possesses."

Then He spoke a parable to them, saying: "The ground of a certain rich man yielded plentifully.' And he thought within himself, saying 'What shall I do, since I have no room to store my crops.'

"So he said, 'I will do this: I will pull down my barns and build greater, and there I will store all my crops and my goods. And I will say to my soul, "Soul, you have many goods laid up for many years; take your ease; eat, drink and be merry."'

"But God said to him, 'Fool! This night your soul will be required of you; then whose will those things be which you have provided?"

"So is he who lays up treasure for himself, and is not rich toward God."

Think About: What lessons should we learn from this parable?

_____

_____

_____

_____

1) **Tomorrow is not guaranteed.** God called the rich man a fool because he lived for himself and trusted his wealth. However, all of his wealth was unable to buy him another day on Earth.

2) **Any wealth that is not used wisely can be taken in an instant.** The rich man was not able to take his wealth with him. He left all his worldly possessions behind for another to enjoy.

3) **God will put the arrogant in their place.** The rich man did not concern himself with the needs of others. Instead, he spent his wealth on his leisure and comfort. He became proud and arrogant of the wealth he had accumulated. Therefore, God decided to take it all from him.

4) **Wealth provides no eternal security.** The rich man did not build treasure in Heaven, and he did not put his trust in the Lord. Therefore, he is not spending eternity in Heaven. Sadly, the rich fool received what he had prepared for himself--an eternity in hell.

Wealth can make your life on Earth more pleasant, but it cannot give you eternal security unless given back to God and used for His purposes. May we all take to heart the lessons of the rich fool and put our faith and trust in God rather than money.

Additional Insights into the Frivolity of Wealth

There are many more verses that speak to the frivolity of putting our trust in wealth. A few of them are listed below. Look up the verses in the NKJV and fill-in the missing words. Read them and ask God to help you place your trust in Him and not in wealth.

Proverbs 11:4 Riches do not _____ in the day of wrath, but _____ delivers from death.

Ecclesiastes 5:13 – 14 There is a severe _____ which I have seen under the sun: _____ kept for their owner to his _____. But those riches _____ through _____; when he begets a son, there is _____ in his hand.

Proverbs 27:24 For _____ are not _____, nor does a _____ endure for all _____.

Proverbs 15:16 Better is a _____ with the fear of the Lord, than great _____ with trouble.

Life Application:

Proverbs 23: 4 – 5 instructs us, *"Do not wear yourself out to get rich; do not trust your own cleverness. Cast but a glance at riches, and they are gone, for they will surely sprout wings and fly off to the sky like an eagle." (NIV)*

This verse reminds us not to make wealth the goal of our life's work. Our goal should be to honor God in all that we do. God may or may not choose to bless us with riches, but He promises to meet all our needs.

This verse also reinforces that we are not to put our trust in riches or our own cleverness. In the last economic crisis, wealth was lost quickly as home values plunged, retirement accounts lost 40 percent of their value or more, and some "sure-fire" investments were revealed to be fraudulent schemes.

Commit this week to re-organize your priorities according to God's word. Making money and becoming financially successful should not be at the top of your list. Consider what priorities will bring the most honor to God and true contentment to your life.

Priorities List:

_____

_____

_____

_____

_____

_____

_____

LESSON 4

God's Provision and Our Obedience

In this lesson, we will look at how God provides for us and what He asks of us in return.

God Provides for His People

Every day God is providing for us. We do not always acknowledge His provisions, and often we are not even consciously aware of the many ways God provides for us. Some financial blessings are quite apparent--you receive an unexpected check in the mail, or someone treats your family to lunch. Others are less evident--you discover a small leak in your roof before it becomes a significant problem, a bill is less than you expected, or many of the items on your shopping list are on sale this week. It is common to think of these "smaller" blessings as coincidences or good luck. Yet, they are indeed blessings from God. You should strive to take note of these blessings and remember to thank God for them.

While Steve was unemployed, I kept a journal of unexpected ways that God blessed us financially. Some of these blessings were:

- Steve received an unexpected Christmas bonus from his employer two weeks before being laid off.

- We had made our last college tuition payment for our son while Steve was still employed.
- We received money back from two bills which I had mistakenly paid twice.
- My father accidentally hit my garage with his car; the insurance payment far exceeded the charge to have the garage repaired.
- The federal government added $25 a week to unemployment benefits, bringing Steve's benefits to 25 percent of his salary.

In Deuteronomy 6, God instructed the Israelites to create testimonies of God's faithfulness to them so that they could teach future generations regarding His blessings. Journaling is one way to keep a record of God's faithfulness to share with your children and grandchildren.

Activity: Think about specific ways you have observed God providing for you and your family. Jot down a few as a record of God's faithfulness. This record of God's faithfulness will serve to increase your faith when you walk through times of trouble.

_____

_____

_____

_____

God's provisions are not always financial--God provides words of encouragement, helping hands, open and closed doors, solutions to difficult problems, and other clear demonstrations of His love when we need them. I encourage you to record those provisions in your journal, as well.

Activity: Write down some ways God has provided for you in nonfinancial ways.

_____

_____

_____

_____

_____

_____

Read Deuteronomy 8:17 – 18.

"You may say to yourself, 'My power and the strength of my hands have produced this wealth for me.' But remember the Lord your God, for it is he who gives you the ability to produce wealth, ..." (NIV)

> ➤ What does this verse tell us about the way God provides for us?

_____

_____

It is God who gives us our mental and physical abilities. Without His grace and provision, we are unable to accomplish anything. I am always pleased when I hear athletes, actors, songwriters, and other celebrities thanking God for their talent. Although they had to work hard to achieve their successes, they could not have accomplished what they did without God giving them the talents and skills. Like them, we should daily acknowledge that it is only through God's provisions for us that we can work to provide for our families.

Although many athletes and performers do acknowledge that their abilities are God-given, many others do not. In their arrogance, they want all the credit for themselves. Of course, one does not have to achieve celebrity-status to become proud and arrogant. We display pride and arrogance when we think of ourselves as better than our neighbors because we have passed a test, earned a degree, or received a promotion. When I hear people boasting of their achievements, King Nebuchadnezzar's arrogance comes to mind. He paid a high price for his arrogance.

The fourth chapter of Daniel tells Nebuchadnezzar's story. God had warned the king in a dream, which Daniel interpreted for him, that he was guilty of self-righteousness. Daniel counseled the king to repent and humble himself. Nebuchadnezzar did not heed Daniel's warning. Daniel 4:30 quotes the king as saying, *"Is not this the great Babylon I have built as the royal residence, by my mighty power and for the glory of my majesty?"* (NIV) As he spoke the words, God took away his sanity and drove him to live like an animal in the fields. God restored Nebuchadnezzar's mind and returned him to the throne after the king repented.

Nebuchadnezzar's story is an extreme example. Yet, it is easy to think of many instances where a sudden misfortune has humbled the arrogant. We have all heard of elite athletes who have been crippled by spinal cord injuries or brilliant scientists who have lost their intellectual abilities due to strokes or Alzheimer's disease. Our physical and mental skills are not guaranteed and should never be taken for granted. We need to remember that God gives us the ability to work and produce wealth, and we need to be grateful to Him for those abilities.

As you read the following Bible verses, think about what each verse tells us about God's provisions for His people.

➢ **Psalm 37:25**

"I have been young, and now am old; yet I have not seen the righteous forsaken, Nor his descendants begging bread."

_____

_____

➢ **Matthew 7:7 – 8**

"Ask, and it will be given to you; seek, and you will find; knock, and it will be opened to you. For everyone who asks receives, and he who seeks finds, and to him who knocks, it will be opened."

_____

_____

We need to trust God for our provisions. These verses are just two of the many times in God's word that He promises that His people will never go without food, and He will provide for us when we ask Him.

God wants us to ask Him for what we need and to thank Him when He meets our needs. Ask the Holy Spirit to help you become more aware of the many ways God blesses you financially each week and make a habit to acknowledge these blessings and thank God for them.

Lesson from the Old Testament: The Widow and Elijah

Read the story about the widow and Elijah from I Kings 17:7 – 16. As you read this story, consider what we can learn from this story regarding God's provision for His people.

And it happened after a while that the brook dried up, because there had been no rain in the land.

Then the word of the Lord came to him, saying, "Arise, go to Zarephath, which belongs to Sidon, and dwell there. See, I have commanded a widow there to provide for you." So he arose and went to Zarephath. And when he came to the gate of the city, indeed a widow was there gathering sticks. And he called to her and said, "Please bring me a little water in a cup, that I may drink." And as she was going to get it, he called to her and said, "Please bring me a morsel of bread in your hand."

So she said, "As the Lord your God lives, I do not have bread, only a handful of flour in a bin, and a little oil in a jar; and see, I am gathering a couple of sticks that I may go in and prepare it for myself and my son, that we may eat it, and die."

And Elijah said to her, "Do not fear; go and do as you have said, but make me a small cake from it first, and bring it to me; and afterward make some for yourself and your son. For thus says the Lord God of Israel: 'The bin of flour shall not be used up, nor shall the jar of oil run dry, until the day the Lord sends rain on the earth.'"

So she went away and did according to the word of Elijah; and she and he and her household ate for many days. The bin of flour was not used up, nor did the jar of oil run dry, according to the word of the Lord which He spoke by Elijah.

Think About: What can we learn from this illustration about God's provision?

_____

_____

_____

_____

_____

_____

When I read this story, it reminds me that:

> ➤ God does provide for His people. Elijah was God's servant, and God provided for his needs. Before he even had a need, God had a plan to provide for him.
> ➤ God wants us to trust Him. Both Elijah and the widow had to trust that God was going to provide for them. They both demonstrated their confidence in God by obeying His commands.
> ➤ We need to give to the work of the Lord first and then take care of ourselves. Elijah instructed the widow to see to his needs before seeing to her own. This request was a test of faith. Because the widow trusted God and obeyed, God met her needs and Elijah's needs until the Lord ended the famine by sending rain.

We Give Back to God's Work

God provides for all of our needs, and He expects us to trust Him and to obey Him. This obedience includes following His instructions to tithe and to care for those in need.

What do the following verses tell us about giving back to the Lord?

➤ **1 Samuel 15:22**

"So Samuel said: 'Has the Lord as great delight in burnt offerings and sacrifices, As in obeying the voice of the Lord? Behold, to obey is better than sacrifice, and to heed is better than the fat of rams.'"

God desires _____

The Israelites were trying to keep God's favor by bringing sacrifices and burnt offerings while disobeying His instructions to refrain from participating in their neighbors' evil practices. Samuel was telling the people that offerings are not enough.

➤ **1 Corinthians 16:1 – 2**

"Now about the collection for the Lord's people…On the first day of every week, each one of you should set aside a sum of money in keeping with his income." (NIV)

This verse tells us that we are to _____.

The amount we give should be based on _____.

In this passage, Paul instructs Christians to provide for those who do God's work. Paul does not ask that each person give equally, but they are to give in proportion to their income. Paul's idea supports the concept of tithing, in which everyone gives ten percent (10%) of their income to the work of the church.

➤ **Exodus 25:2**

"Tell the Israelites to bring me an offering. You are to receive the offering for me from everyone whose heart prompts them to give." (NIV)

HONORING GOD WITH YOUR MONEY

We should give _____.

Giving should be done willingly and with a proper attitude toward God. If someone gives grudgingly, God will not accept his or her offering.

Think About: The following verses instruct us on how we are to give and how much we are to give. Look up the verses and fill in the missing words (NKJV). As you do, think about how we can honor God through our giving.

2 Chronicles 24:10 Then all the _____ and all the people _____, brought their contributions, and put them in the chest until _____ had been given.

2 Chronicles 31:12 Then they _____ brought in the _____, the tithes, and the dedicated _____.

Proverbs 3:9 – 10 _____ the Lord with your possessions, and with the _____ of all your increase; so your barns will be filled with _____, and your vats will _____ with new wine.

Exodus 35:21 Then everyone came whose heart was _____ and everyone whose _____ was willing, and they brought the Lord's _____ for the work of the tabernacle of meeting, for all its _____, and for the holy garments.

2 Corinthians 8:12 For if there is first a _____ mind, it is accepted according to what one _____, and not according to what he does _____ have."

➢ What types of offerings should we give? (Refer to 2 Chronicles 31:12 above).

_____

_____

➢ What is the difference between an offering and a tithe?

_____

_____

➢ Read Malachi 3:8 – 10 and 2 Corinthians 9:10 – 11 below. If we follow God's commands, what does He promise us?

_____

_____

Malachi 3:8 – 10

"Will a man rob God? Yet you have robbed Me! But you say, 'In what way have we robbed You?' In tithes and offerings. You are cursed with a curse, For you have robbed Me, Even this whole nation. Bring all the tithes into the storehouse, That there may be food in My house, And try Me now in this," Says the Lord of hosts, "If I will not open for you the windows of heaven, And pour out for you such blessing that there will not be room enough to receive it."

2 Corinthians 9:10 – 11 (NIV)

"Now He who supplies seed to the sower and bread for food will also supply and increase your store of seed and will enlarge the harvest of your righteousness. You will be enriched in every way so that you can be generous on every occasion, and through us your generosity will result in thanksgiving to God."

Giving according to what we have—typically ten percent, or a tithe, of our income--ensures that everyone is contributing, but no one is unduly burdened.

Furthermore, 2 Chronicles 31:12 (see above) instructs us to give tithes, contributions, and dedicated gifts. Tithes are the first ten percent of our income that belongs to God. Contributions are gifts above our tithes. Dedicated gifts are to meet a specific purpose.

Out of obedience to God, we should give to the church's work. Furthermore, we should have a thankful heart for the many blessings He gives us. God also promised to bless those who tithe extravagantly and those who provide for His work.

Missions Faith Pledge: Steve and I were graduate students for the first few years of our marriage. Money was tight, but we were faithful in tithing. In the fall of 1983, our church had a missions conference and encouraged each member to make a Missions Faith Pledge. Steve and I strongly felt that we should pledge $15 a month, even though this would strain our already tight budget. We filled out the card and asked the Lord to provide the money. A few days later, I was notified that I had won the grand prize in a local shopping center contest. I received a gift certificate from nearly every shop in the center. The value of the gift was more than the $180 we had pledged for the coming year. We had not committed the $15 a month with the expectation of receiving such a tangible gift. However, the winnings confirmed to us that God was rewarding our obedience and that when we obey God with our finances, He does *"pour out for you such blessing that there will not be room enough to receive it."* (Malachi 3:10)

Life Application:

2 Corinthians 9:6 – 7 *"But this I say: He who sows sparingly will also reap sparingly, and he who sows bountifully will also reap bountifully. So let each one give as he purposes in his heart, not grudgingly or of necessity; for God loves a cheerful giver."*

God instructed the Israelites to record His blessings and faithfulness to teach future generations and serve as a reminder to them in dark times. We need to do this also.

Assignment: Purchase a journal this week and begin recording God's blessings. Share your journal entries regularly with your children. Or better yet, make journaling a family activity. Encourage each family member to share ways they have noticed God providing for your family and then record each observation. Make a habit of thanking God daily for the blessings He has given to you and your family. When your attitude is one of gratefulness to God, it will be much easier to fulfill the command above to sow bountifully and to give cheerfully.

Business Practices that Honor God

Our dealings and interactions with others in business—whether our employers, our employees, our co-workers, or those serving us—need to reflect Christian principles of fairness and honesty. This lesson examines what the Bible says about fair business practices and its warnings against dishonesty.

Think About: Do you reflect Christ in the way you treat those with whom you do business? In the way that you treat your co-workers or your employees? Do you honor God in the way you treat store clerks and restaurant servers? Take a moment to ask God to reveal how your actions in this area please Him and places you need to improve.

Treatment of Employees

Think About: The following verses provide instructions on how we should treat those who work for us. Look up the verses and fill in the missing words (NKJV). As you do, consider whether you treat your employees, if any, as God commands. Are you being treated fairly by your employer?

Leviticus 19:13b The _____ of him who is hired shall not _____ with you all night until morning.

Deuteronomy 24:15 Each day you shall give him his _____, and not let the sun go down on it, for he is _____ and has his _____ set on it; lest he cry out _____ you to the Lord, and it be _____ to you.

Isaiah 58:3 "Why have we _____", they say, "and You have not seen? Why have we _____ our souls, and You take no notice?" In fact, in the day of your fast you find_____, and _____ all your laborers."

Malachi 3:5 And I will come near you for _____; I will be a swift _____ against sorcerers, against adulterers, against perjurers, against those who exploit _____ earners and widows and _____, and against those who turn away an _____--because they do not fear Me, says the Lord of hosts.

James 5:4 Indeed the _____ of the laborers who mowed your fields, which you kept back by _____, cry out; and the _____ of the reapers have reached the _____ of the Lord of Sabaoth.

Lesson from the Teachings of Christ: The Parable of the Workers in the Vineyard

As we saw in the verses above, the Bible commands that employers should treat workers justly and pay them a fair wage when it is due. Most of the scriptures on the subject of workers agree with our current employment practices and law. However, the Parable of the Workers in the Vineyard does not seem to fit our fairness ideas. As you read this parable below, try to imagine yourself as one of the characters in this story and how you might feel.

Matthew 20:1 – 16

"For the kingdom of heaven is like a landowner who went out early in the morning to hire laborers for his vineyard. Now when he had agreed with the

laborers for a denarius a day, he sent them into his vineyard. And he went out about the third hour and saw others standing idle in the marketplace, and said to them, 'You also go into the vineyard, and whatever is right I will give you.' So they went. Again he went out about the sixth and the ninth hour, and did likewise. And about the eleventh hour he went out and found others standing idle, and said to them, 'Why have you been standing here idle all day?' They said to him, 'Because no one hired us.' He said to them, 'You also go into the vineyard, and whatever is right you will receive.'

"So when evening had come, the owner of the vineyard said to his steward, 'Call the laborers and give them their wages, beginning with the last to the first.' And when those came who were hired about the eleventh hour, they each received a denarius. But when the first came, they supposed that they would receive more; and they likewise received each a denarius. And when they had received it, they complained against the landowner, saying, 'These last men have worked only one hour, and you made them equal to us who have borne the burden and the heat of the day.' But he answered one of them and said, 'Friend, I am doing you no wrong. Did you not agree with me for a denarius? Take what is yours and go your way. I wish to give to this last man the same as to you. Is it not lawful for me to do what I wish with my own things? Or is your eye evil because I am good?' So the last will be first, and the first last. For many are called, but few chosen."

➢ How would you feel if you were one of the first workers to be hired?

_____

_____

➢ What if you were the last worker hired?

_____

_____

➢ What are the implications of this story for how we treat workers?

_____

_____

➢ Do our laws prevent this type of generosity from an employer?

_____

_____

If you were the last worker hired, your attitude likely would be one of extreme gratitude. All-day long, those workers had waited for someone to offer them employment. Each time an employer showed up, I am sure they prayed to be among the chosen. The last workers needed a job just as severely as the first workers hired. They had families who needed food and provision. When the employer finally called them over and offered them work, I am sure they were grateful for the opportunity but were expecting only an hour's pay. Their hearts must have swelled with thankfulness when the employer paid them a full day's wage.

I believe that Jesus described an employer who looked at each worker with compassion and saw the desire of his heart to provide for his family. The employer did not intend to hurt those who worked a full day, but he wanted to give the same blessing to those hired later in the day. Today our employment laws prevent employers from treating workers differently. However, the law does not prevent employers from being generous with employees who need assistance.

One way an employer can honor God with her money is to ask God to show her which employees are hurting financially and look for ways to bless those individuals. An employer might provide an employee with an opportunity to work overtime and earn extra money. She might give additional training and money for college classes to help an employee to advance into a higher paying job. If the employee's need is urgent, God might instruct the employer to personally provide the funds to meet the need or direct the employee to churches and agencies that assist.

An employer who seeks to honor God with her money will find many opportunities to bless her workers and improve their lives. In turn, God will bless that employer and allow her to create more jobs to provide more people with employment.

Employees as Faithful Stewards

We have seen that God's Word instructs employers to treat their employees fairly and pay them their wages on time. In return, the Bible also talks about how workers should interact with their bosses-commanding workers to submit to their bosses and be faithful stewards of what is entrusted to them.

Read Mathew 24: 45 – 47

"Who then is a faithful and wise servant, whom his master made ruler over his household, to give them food in due season? Blessed is that servant whom his master, when he comes, will find so doing. Assuredly, I say to you that he will make him ruler over all his goods"

> ➢ How should an employee behave when his boss is not around?

_____

_____

> ➢ If you work faithfully and wisely, what should you expect from your boss?

_____

_____

Jesus is commanding us, as workers, to work hard for our employers, even when the boss is not present. Those employees who diligently do their work and make the right decisions for their employers are the ones who will be promoted and given more responsibilities. Of course, we have all heard of situations where this has not happened, but this is generally the case.

Think About: Maybe you are in a situation in which you are not treated fairly at work. Are you still obligated to do your best work and try to make your boss look good?

_____

_____

_____

It is easy to work hard for a great boss, but much more challenging to do so when your boss takes advantage of you and does not treat you fairly. However, we must remember that as Christians, our behavior should always reflect and honor God.

Read 1 Peter 2:18 – 19

"Servants, be submissive to your masters with all fear, not only to the good and gentle, but also to the harsh. For this is commendable, if because of conscience toward God one endures grief, suffering wrongfully."

> ➢ What should our attitudes be toward our employers?

_____

_____

➢ Should our behavior depend on how our employers treat us?

_____

_____

➢ Why are we to submit to our employers?

_____

_____

Think About: The way you interact with your boss can reflect Christ's teachings and honor God, or it can hurt your testimony and fail to glorify God. The following is a guide for a Christian employee. The verses instruct workers so they can honor God through their behavior and attitudes while they work. Look up the scriptures in the NKJV and fill-in the missing words. As you do so, ask God to help you have a proper attitude toward your employer.

1 Timothy 6:1 Let as many _____ as are under the yoke count their own _____ worthy of all _____, so that the name of God and His doctrine may not be _____.

Colossians 3:22 – 24 Bondservants, _____ in all things your _____ according to the flesh, not with _____, as men-pleasers, but in sincerity of _____, fearing God. And whatever you do, do it _____, as to the Lord and not to men, knowing that from the _____ you will receive the _____ of the inheritance; for you _____ the Lord Christ.

Titus 2:9 – 10 Exhort bondservants to be _____ to their own masters, to be well _____ in all things, not _____ back, not _____, but showing all good _____, that they may adorn the _____ of God our Savior in all things.

Other Business Dealings

Tipping

These days, it is relatively common to see stories about customers who refused to tip servers or left ill-mannered messages on their bills. Some of those customers profess to be Christians, and one highly-publicized story involved a pastor. The pastor was part of a large group; the restaurant added an automatic 18 percent gratuity, per its stated policy, to each bill. The pastor crossed out the tip and wrote, "I give God 10 percent. Why do you get 18." The angry server posted the receipt on the Internet, to which many people reacted. Many of those who commented were servers who complained about how poorly Christians generally tip.

I was very disappointed by this pastor's behavior and the behaviors described in the article's comments. I have been a waitress, and I find much truth in the negative comments about Christian tipping. I can recall a large group of about twelve that came to the restaurant each Sunday after their evening service. The group typically arrived about 20 minutes before closing, ordered coffee and dessert, and stayed for nearly an hour after closing time. They seemed oblivious to the fact that the restaurant had closed and that the server had to wait for them to leave. However, each week they were politely served and allowed to linger as long as they wanted. In return, the group collectively left a tip of $2 - $3. Consequently, no server wanted to get stuck with their table. Their behavior did not honor Christ.

Indeed, some customers who refuse to tip are responding to poor customer service or are protesting our system of tipping those who serve us. The Bible does not explicitly address tipping. Nevertheless, it has plenty to say about treating others fairly, especially those who work for us. Those who provide a service are, in a sense, our employees during the time of their service. Service industry professionals include hairstylists, restaurant servers, drivers, and food delivery persons. Many of these workers are paid a fraction of minimum wage and depend on tips to make a reasonable living. You may disagree with the system; however, that does not give you the right to deny a tip to someone who has served you. The size of your tip may reflect your feelings about the quality of the service you received.

Activity: Re-read Malachi 3:5 from above and James 5:4 as re-written below.

"Indeed the wages of the laborers who serve you, which you have kept back by fraud, cry out; the cries of the servers have reached the ears of the Lord of Sabaoth."

➢ What mental picture do you get when you think about "laborers?"

_____

_____

➢ Merriam-Webster.com defines a laborer as "a person who does unskilled physical work for wages." What do these verses tell you about how you should treat people who "work for wages?"

_____

_____

➢ Restaurant servers, door attendants, cab drivers, and baggage handlers fit this definition. Even some skilled workers, such as hairdressers, work for tips. If the tips they receive from their customers are part of their wages, what do these verses tell us about tipping?

_____

_____

> Think about the way you treat those who serve you. How can you honor Christ through your treatment of them? Do you consider your Christian testimony when you decide how much to tip?

_____

_____

Collecting Debts and Interest

Think About: The following verses concern the collection of money owed to you and the charging of interest. Look up the verses and fill in the missing words (NKJV). As you do, consider what the Bible says about business practices.

Exodus 22:25 If you lend _____ to any of My people who are _____ among you, you shall not be like a _____ to him; you shall not charge him _____.

Proverbs 13:11 _____ gained by _____ will be diminished. But he who _____ by labor will increase.

Proverbs 28:8 One who increases his _____ by _____ and _____ gathers it for him who will pity the _____.

Luke 3:13 – 14 And he said to them, "_____ no more than what is _____ for you…be _____ with your wages.

These verses make it clear that God expects His people to be fair and honest in all their business interactions. If God directs you to lend money to someone in need, you should do so without charging them a high-interest rate. Lending money to a hurting brother or sister should not be for your profit. God also warns against collecting more money than is due to you.

Lesson from the Teachings of Christ: The Parable of the Shrewd Manager

As I developed this Bible study, the parable of the Shrewd Manager did not seem to agree with my sense of reasoning, yet I strongly sensed that I should include it.

Luke 16: 1 – 9

He also said to His disciples: "There was a certain rich man who had a steward, and an accusation was brought to him that this man was wasting his goods. So he called him and said to him, 'What is this I hear about you? Give an account of your stewardship, for you can no longer be steward.'

"Then the steward said within himself, 'What shall I do? For my master is taking the stewardship away from me. I cannot dig; I am ashamed to beg. I have resolved what to do, that when I am put out of the stewardship, they may receive me into their houses.'

"So he called every one of his master's debtors to him, and said to the first, 'How much do you owe my master?' And he said, 'A hundred measures of oil.' So he said to him, 'Take your bill, and sit down quickly and write fifty.' Then he said to another, 'And how much do you owe?' So he said, 'A hundred measures of wheat.' And he said to him, 'Take your bill, and write eighty.' So the master commended the unjust steward because he had dealt shrewdly. For the sons of this world are more shrewd in their generation than the sons of light.

"And I say to you, make friends for yourselves by unrighteous mammon, that when you fail, they may receive you into an everlasting home.

➤ How do you feel about the behavior of the manager?

_____

_____

➤ Would you have commended the manager if you were the master?

_____

_____

➤ Are you surprised by Jesus's comment in verse 9?

_____

_____

When I taught this lesson in a Sunday school class, someone read a commentary that suggested that the manager had been cheating the customers, and he changed the bills back to what was owed to the master. There is certainly reason to believe that might be true, as we know from Zacchaeus's story that tax collectors frequently charged people more tax than was owed and kept the difference for themselves. So, it may be the manager was undoing his wrongs and was, thus, praised by his master.

I found the final statement to be the most surprising, *"I tell you, use worldly wealth to gain friends for yourselves, so that when it is gone, you will be welcomed into eternal dwellings."* (NIV) I am quite sure that Jesus is not advocating "buying" our way into Heaven, but I did not have a clear understanding of the passage. So, I looked up several commentaries on this passage to assist me in understanding what Jesus was saying. They all made the point that Jesus was addressing the Pharisees. The Pharisees had placed heavy burdens on the ordinary people to bring more money into the temple and support their lavish lifestyles. The explanation that I found to be the clearest comes from Hillschurch.blogspot.com:

"The Jewish priests and rulers (Sanhedrin) should be using their wealth and influence (even though it belongs to God) to be blessing others (making friends) so that they are able to secure eternal blessings (literally an eternal dwelling place) not just to be comfortable here on earth. The wealth of God is to be used to lavishly bless people, not to hoard it to yourselves or to be stored in barns – even if the barn is the temple."[1]

Jesus was pointing out that they needed to share their wealth with the poor and needy so that God would one day welcome them into Heaven. That explanation is consistent with the other scriptures we have read on treating others fairly and using our wealth to bless others rather than hoarding it for ourselves.

I particularly like the Bible translation of this parable from *The Message*. The final portion from that version reads, *"The master praised the crooked manager! And why? Because he knew how to look after himself. Streetwise people are smarter in this regard than law-abiding citizens. They are on constant alert, looking for angles, surviving by their wits. I want you to be smart in the same way--but for what is right--using every adversity to stimulate you to creative survival, to concentrate your attention on the bare essentials, so you'll live, really live, and not complacently just get by on good behavior."*

Satan is working hard to lure Christians into sin. He is devious and often uses "good" things to trap us. Like the wise manager, we have to be alert and shrewd to avoid the devil's traps. Money is one of the primary tools Satan uses to entrap people. He is sly enough to use both a lack of money and an excess of money as tools to lead us astray. One way we can avoid Satan's traps is to remember that we are only stewards of the wealth God has entrusted to us. It all belongs to Him, and we need to use it according to His purposes. If we truly honor God with our money, Satan cannot get a foothold in that area of our lives.

Think About: What does this parable say to you? Does it inspire you to improve your money management? Does it inspire you to live in a more Christ-like manner?

_____

_____

_____

_____

Life Application:

Jesus followed the parable of the Shrewd Manager with the verses I chose for this lesson's life application: *"He who is faithful in what is least is faithful also in much; and he who is unjust in what is least is unjust also in much. Therefore if you have not been faithful in the unrighteous mammon, who will commit to your trust the true riches? And if you have not been faithful in what is another man's, who will give you what is your own? (Luke 16: 10 – 12)*

God expects us to manage, to the best of our abilities, the assets He has given us. He also expects us to manage well any assets others entrust to us. If we properly oversee what God gives us, He can trust us with more. And as we have seen in earlier lessons, He gives to us abundantly so that we, in turn, can bless others.

Activity: Pray diligently and consider how you might be a better steward of the assets God has given to you. These steps might include balancing your checkbook regularly, tracking your spending, cleaning out your closets, sharing your unneeded clothing with those who can use them, praying about significant spending decisions, and creating a budget.

Make a list of steps you can take to manage the assets God has given you in ways that honor Him.

_____

_____

_____

_____

_____

_____

_____

_____

_____

Note:

[1] http://hillschurch.blogspot.com/2008/08/parable-of-shrewd-manager.html, August 12, 2008.

Honoring God through Work and Charitable Giving

In this lesson, we consider what the Bible says about the value of work and God's commands regarding charity.

Commands to Work

Think About: In the following scripture verses, we see that God expects non-disabled individuals to work and provide for their families. Look up the verses and fill in the missing words (NKJV).

Proverbs 10:4 He who has a slack hand becomes _____, but the hand of the _____ makes _____.

Proverbs 21:17 He who loves _____ will be a _____ man; he who loves wine and oil will not be _____.

Proverbs 28:19 – 20 He who tills his land will have _____ of bread, but he who follows _____ will have _____ enough! A _____ man will abound with _____, but he who hastens to be _____ will not go _____.

Clearly, God expects everyone who can work to work. God requires us to take care of those who cannot provide for their own needs, but we cannot enable those who are unwilling to work to be lazy and profit from our labors. God promises that if we are diligent and work, we will have the food we need. On the other hand, if we choose to engage in laziness and pleasure-seeking, God warns us of a life of poverty. Please realize that we are not to work to get rich. God promises punishment to those seeking riches, and He promises blessings to those who use the wealth He entrusts to them to honor Him (Proverbs 28:19 – 20).

Commands to be Generous with the Poor

Think About: We are to work and support ourselves and our families. However, God also commands us to be generous and share with the poor. As you complete the following verses, think about how the verses reveal how God expects us to treat the poor.

Deuteronomy 15:7 If there is among you a poor man…you shall not _____ your _____ nor shut your _____ from your poor brother.

Deuteronomy 15:11 For the _____ will never cease from the land; therefore I command you, saying "You shall open your hand _____ to your brother, to your poor and your _____, in your land.

Deuteronomy 26:12 When you have finished laying aside all the _____ of your increase in the third year—the year of _____ --and have given it to the Levite, the _____, the _____ and the _____, so that they may eat within your gates and be filled.

Leviticus 19:10 And you shall not _____ your vineyard, nor shall you _____ every grape of your _____; you shall leave them for the _____ and the _____. I am the Lord your God.

HONORING GOD WITH YOUR MONEY

Luke 14:13 – 14 But when you give a _____, invite the poor, the maimed, the _____, the _____. And you will be _____, because they cannot _____ you; for you shall be repaid at the resurrection of the _____."

> ➤ To which specific groups of people are we commanded to show generosity?

1) _____
2) _____
3) _____
4) _____
5) _____
6) _____

God commands that we show generosity to several groups of people. The first tenth of our income should be given to our church to support the church's work, including paying the pastor a reasonable salary. He also tells us to be generous with those who cannot care for themselves—orphans, widows, and the disabled. In the New Testament, Paul clarifies that the church should help those who have no family to care for them. Also, the widows of marriageable age should be encouraged to remarry rather than receive support from the church.

God also commands His people to care for the poor and foreigners. Deuteronomy 15:11 tells us, *"there will always be poor people in the land."* Remember that God decides who will be rich and who will be poor, and He expects wealthy people to be generous with those who are not. God also reminded the Israelites that they were foreigners when they entered the Promised Land, and they should show generosity to foreigners. Our country has always been a melting pot of foreigners. America receives about a million immigrants a year, and God tells us in scripture to treat them with fairness and generosity.

Read the following verses:

2 Corinthians 9:11 *"You will be enriched in every way so that you can be generous on every occasion, and through us your generosity will result in thanksgiving to God." (NIV)*

Proverbs 19:17 *"He who has pity on the poor lends to the Lord, and He will pay back what he has given."*

> ➤ What does God promise to those who are generous?

_____

_____

Read the following verses.

Proverbs 17:5 *"He who mocks the poor reproaches his Maker; he who is glad at calamity will not go unpunished."*

Proverbs 21:13 *"Whoever shuts his ears to the cry of the poor will also cry himself and not be heard."*

Proverbs 28:27 *"He who gives to the poor will not lack, but he who hides his eyes will have many curses."*

> ➤ What does God promise to those who do not assist the poor?

_____

_____

_____

Lesson from the New Testament: Story of Cornelius

Acts 10:1 – 4

> *At Caesarea, there was a man named Cornelius, a centurion in what was known as the Italian Regiment. He and all his family were devout and God-fearing; he gave generously to those in need and prayed to God regularly. One day at about three in the afternoon he had a vision. He distinctly saw an angel of God, who came to him and said, "Cornelius!"*
>
> *Cornelius stared at him in fear. "What is it, Lord?" he asked.*
>
> *The angel answered, "Your prayers and gifts to the poor have come up as a memorial offering before God."*

➤ What did Cornelius do that attracted God's attention?

_____

_____

➤ What characteristics of Cornelius's life should we emulate?

_____

_____

As this story continues, God instructs Peter to go to Cornelius, a Gentile, and share the good news of Jesus Christ with him. Cornelius's generosity and devotion to doing good deeds did not save him. Salvation can come only through faith in Jesus Christ. However, God singled him out to be the first Gentile with whom Peter shared the gospel because of his generosity. From the story, we should learn that God expects us to give generously to the poor and that God answers the prayers of those devoted to Him and who spend time regularly in prayer.

Guidelines for Charitable Giving

I once read a definition of debt as "excessive charity." My initial reaction was to disagree with the statement, as I tend to think of debt resulting from either living beyond one's means or from hardships, such as losing a job. I had never considered that some people might be in debt due to giving away too much of their money. I am unsure what portion of America's debt-riddled masses might have gotten into that state through excessive charity. I am still inclined to believe that most consumer debt results from the desire to "have our cake now and pay for it later" and the hardships that have been imposed by our recent and ongoing economic disruptions.

Nevertheless, examining when to give to charity and how much to donate is an integral part of our discussion. The Bible clarifies that those who have excess resources are to share with those less fortunate than themselves. Many people are tempted to give to every deserving cause. Furthermore, there are numerous charities to which we feel obligated to donate. In fact, the IRS reports that there are 1.5 million tax-exempt organizations in the United States. They each represent a "good" cause that we might be tempted to support. In order to protect our budgets and not go into debt through giving, it is crucial to have a plan for giving and standards to determine the causes or groups to which one will donate.

Keep in mind that tithing is the first priority and is not optional. God directs us to tithe one-tenth of our income to the work of the church. Giving to other charities should be above and beyond tithing. God distinguished tithes from other giving, as in Deuteronomy 12:11 (NIV), *"Then to the place the Lord your God will choose as a dwelling for his Name—there you are to bring everything I command you: your burnt offerings and sacrifices, your tithes and special gifts, and all the choice possessions you have vowed to the Lord."*

Here are some considerations to keep in mind when planning charitable donations:

1) **Meet the needs of your own family before giving to others.** Paul provides instructions for charitable giving in 1 Timothy Chapter 5. He

clarifies that those in need should first seek help from their family members before asking others for help. In verse 4, he wrote, *"But if any widow has children or grandchildren, let them first learn to show piety at home and to repay their parents, for this is good and acceptable before God."* In verse 8 of that chapter, Paul had harsh words for those who do not meet the needs of their family, *"If anyone who does not provide for his own, and especially for those of his household, he has denied the faith and is worse than an unbeliever."*

2) **Determine what you can afford to give.** Everyone should include donations to charitable causes in their budget. Those who have excess income should be more generous than those with less. Do not try to out-give others. In 1 Corinthians 16:2 (NIV), Paul reminded us that giving should be based on income, *"On the first day of every week, each one of you should set aside a sum of money in keeping with your income, saving it up, so that when I come no collections will have to be made."*

3) **Give for the right reasons.** The right reason to give is that you identify with the charity and feel led to support it. The wrong reason is to receive the praise of men through recognition and status. Jesus told his followers, *"Therefore, when you do a charitable deed, do not sound a trumpet before you as the hypocrites do in the synagogues and in the streets, that they may have glory from men. Assuredly, I say to you, they have their reward."* (Matthew 6:2)

4) **Pray for God to direct your giving.** As you pray, God will lay burdens on your heart. You cannot give to every good cause. God only expects you to give as He instructs you. In Exodus 25:2 (NIV), God commanded the Israelites to bring an offering. *"You are to receive the offering for me from each man whose heart prompts him to give."*

5) **Give to charities that share your values.** As a Christian, I must wisely use the money God provides for me. This includes supporting charities that further God's kingdom. It also includes giving to organizations that do not directly support our Christian mission but are not in conflict. Such groups might feed the hungry, fund medical research, or help communities recover from a natural disaster.

6) **Seek out charities that have low administrative costs.** Using God's money wisely involves giving to charities that are well-managed and whose administrators are not receiving exorbitant salaries. All tax-exempt charities must reveal what percentage of donations are used for administrative and fundraising expenses. This number should be less than about 15 – 20 percent. The Evangelical Council for Financial Accountability (ecfa.org) accredits churches that responsibly manage their money

I want to encourage you to give generously but within your means. Ask God to direct you to ministries that you can support. I firmly believe that if everyone does their part, then we can meet many needs.

Activity: Make a list of the charities you currently support. Then take time to evaluate if those charities meet the guidelines above. Pray about whether God would have you to continue to support those charities or if He is leading you toward other charities.

_____

_____

_____

_____

_____

_____

Life Application:

Christ gave us instructions on charitable giving in Luke 12:33 – 34 *"Sell what you have and give alms; provide yourself money bags which do not grow old, a treasure in the heavens that does not fail, where no thief approaches nor moth destroys. For where your treasure is, there your heart will be also."*

Think about the treasure you are building. Are you building treasure in Heaven that will last forever or earthly treasure?

This lesson concludes our exploration of what the Bible says about money. In the coming lessons, we will examine practical applications concerning budgeting and living debt-free.

SUSAN E. BALL

Starting Out

Living within your means can be quite challenging when you are young and just starting a life on your own. Steve and I married one week after graduating from college. We had lived at home before marrying and attended our local four-year college. Tuition was affordable, and we graduated with no debt. Then, we moved 800 miles away to pursue our master's degrees. We were buying our groceries and paying rent for the first time in our lives, plus covering the tuition, books, and fees associated with graduate school. Money was tight, and we realized that we had to budget carefully.

Our budget allowed us only $20 per week for food; in today's economy, that would be about $57. We embraced the challenge of planning out meals and shopping for nutritious food without exceeding our budget. We developed a list of about twelve meals that we enjoyed and fit into our financial plan. We often managed to come in $1 or $2 under budget, so we saved that money to splurge occasionally on fancier meals. We supplemented our food budget by growing some of our produce.

We lived in married student housing and paid less than $150 per month on rent (about $427 today), including utilities. The University housing offered many amenities, which helped our budget. With a swimming pool located next to our building, tennis courts nearby, and canoes available to check out for no fee, we could access free activities. The University offered students the opportunity to grow their own vegetables in community gardening plots; we had a large plot in exchange for helping to maintain the common area and walkways. We could walk to class (about 2 miles) or ride the free campus bus. There were many free cultural and sporting events that we could attend. We joined a wonderful church whose members welcomed us warmly; the church offered many ways to connect with people and have fun without spending much money.

In our early days as a married couple, Steve and I learned that we could be quite content with a modest amount of money. We also learned to trust God to meet all our needs. Things were not always easy, but we still had enough food, and we could pay all our bills. We faithfully tithed even during these low-income days. Today, our children are grown, and we both have jobs that pay good salaries. But the lessons we learned on budgeting and living within our means in our early days continue to impact the way we spend, save, and donate our money. As you read the lessons on creating and maintaining a budget and getting out of debt, I pray that the biblical principles Steve and I have learned and employed in our life will help you manage your money well and reduce financial stress. Remember that as you honor God with your finances, He will entrust you with more incredible financial blessings.

LESSON 7

Principles of Budgeting

In our study of how to honor God with our money, we are now entering the practical application phase. In this lesson, we will examine the principles of budgeting. Our focus will shift to applying budgeting principles, useful money management tips, living debt-free, and cultivating real wealth.

Budgeting Principles

1) **Recognize that everything belongs to God**. We are stewards of those possessions that God has entrusted to us. We are obligated to be good and faithful stewards of those possessions.

> **Psalm 24:1** "The earth is the _____, and all its fullness, the _____ and those who dwell therein."

> **Psalm 50: 9 – 12** "I will not take a bull from your house nor goats out of your folds, for every _____ of the forest is Mine, and the _____ on a thousand hills. I know all the birds of the _____, and the wild beasts of the field are Mine. If I were _____, I would not tell you; for the _____ is Mine, and all its fullness."

2) **Tithe**. God asks us to give back the first portion of what He has given us. We should tithe a tenth of our income to do God's work. Take your tithe out of your budget before you begin planning your other expenses. For scriptures on tithing, please refer back to Lesson 4.

3) **Meet the needs of your family.** The largest portion of your budget should go to care for your family's needs, like shelter, food, clothing, transportation, and health care.

> **I Timothy 5:8** "But if anyone does not provide for his _____, and especially for those of his _____, he has denied the faith and is worse than an _____."

4) **Pay debts and obligations.** When you borrow money, you make a promise to repay that money. Borrowed money includes purchases made on credit, as well as educational loans and money borrowed from friends. Christians should strive to honor God by paying all their debts on time and maintaining excellent credit records.

> **Psalm 37:21** "The wicked _____and does not _____, but the righteous shows _____ and gives."

5) **Establish short-term and long-term savings plans.** Short-term savings are for needs anticipated in the coming year, such as vacations, back-to-school clothing, and home furnishings. Long-term savings are to be set aside for retirement, a new home, children's education, and weddings.

> **Proverbs 21:20** "There is desirable _____, and oil in the _____ of the wise, but a foolish man _____ it."

Proverbs 6:6 – 8 "Go to the ant, you _____;
consider her ways and be wise! Which, having no captain,
overseer or ruler, provides her _____
in the summer, and gathers her _____ in
the harvest."

6) **Set aside money for recreation and leisure.** Everyone needs time for relaxation; thus, you should add money for entertainment into your budget. If your money is tight, your leisure activities might need to be free or very low cost. As your income grows, you can plan more costly trips and vacations. God instructed the Israelites to have a day of rest. We also need times of rest.

> **Exodus 16: 29 – 30** "See! For the Lord has given you
> the _____; therefore He gives you on the
> sixth day _____ for two days. Let every man
> remain in his place; let no man go out of place on the
> _____ day." So the people _____
> on the seventh day."

7) **Give money to charitable causes.**

> **Proverbs 22:9** "He who has a _____
> eye will be blessed, for he gives of his _____
> to the _____."

Case Study:

In this lesson, we use MaryAnn and Jason Smith to illustrate these budgeting principles and the problems caused by not following them. Their story is a fictionalized account that demonstrates scenarios I have seen repeated over the many years I have worked with couples to create and use budgets.

MaryAnn and Jason have been married for 18 years. They both have high paying jobs and together earn more than $140,000 annually. Their two children are 12 and 15 years old and are active in school and after-school activities. The Smiths' house payment of $3,200 is high but certainly affordable on their income. The Smiths consider themselves generous and give $6,000 a year to their church and several other charitable causes.

Two years ago, the Smiths refinanced their home to pay off some debts. Now they find themselves with a mortgage, a home equity loan, two car payments, and many credit cards. They pay their bills on time and make substantially more than the minimum payments on their credit cards, so their credit scores are good. However, they have no emergency fund, and their total credit card balances are rising. MaryAnn and Jason often fight about money. Jason thinks MaryAnn spends too much on designer clothing and excessive gifts for the children, whereas MaryAnn thinks Jason's electronic gadget purchases cause their financial stress.

Think About: What budgeting principles have the Smiths failed to follow?

_____

_____

_____

_____

_____

The Smiths are failing in a few areas of the budgeting principles:

1) They have not committed their finances to God. Although they sporadically give money to their church, it was less than 5 percent last year. They should be tithing 10 percent of their income.

2) They are not working together as a team. MaryAnn and Jason both believe that since they work hard and earn high salaries,

they are entitled to spend money on the things they want without consulting their spouse.

3) They have not created a budget, so they do not have an accurate picture of how they spend their money.
4) They have not set aside money for savings and emergencies.
5) They are not paying off their debts each month and are failing to live within their means.

MaryAnn and Jason's errors cause them a great deal of anxiety and create disharmony in their home. God desires that we live without the stress and anxiety that arises when we fail to live within our means. Philippians 4:6 – 7 tells us, *"Be anxious for nothing, but in everything by prayer and supplication, with thanksgiving, let your requests be made known to God; and the peace of God, which surpasses all understanding, will guard your hearts and minds through Christ Jesus."*

Think About: What steps do the Smiths need to take to be more in line with the budgeting principles discussed above?

_____

_____

_____

_____

Jason and MaryAnn have stress and anxiety because they are not following God's commands concerning their money. To get things back on track, MaryAnn and Jason need to:

1) Commit their finances to the Lord. They need to confess that they have been negligent in the handling of their money and repent. Then they need to ask God for wisdom in how to handle their money. God will give them peace and an understanding of how to manage their money.

2) Jason and MaryAnn need to begin tithing immediately. They cannot wait to tithe until they have their finances in order. Tithing while in debt is counterintuitive to our way of thinking; however, God has promised to bless those who tithe.

3) The couple needs to work together to create a budget. It must be a team effort, and it must meet the needs of each of them.

4) The budget must allow each of them some money to spend as they choose. Of course, the amount decided upon must fit within the budget.

5) They must be frugal with any spending on nonessential items until they have paid off all their credit card debt and car loans.

6) They need to set aside a sum of money for expected future expenses and funds to handle emergencies.

The Root of Budget Problems: Attitude

In his book *"Family Budgets That Work,"* Larry Burkett identified "attitude" as the root of financial problems[1] Attitudes that lead to budget problems can manifest themselves as greed, covetousness, ignorance, indulgence, or impatience. The Bible warns us against each of these attitudes. In the following section are the definitions of these terms. Read the descriptions and complete the Scripture verses.

> **Greed** *arises when we have an overwhelming desire for more wealth or possessions than we truly need.* Both King Solomon and Jesus warned about the destructiveness of greed.

Proverbs 1:19 So are the_____ of everyone who is _____for gain; it takes away the _____of its_____.

Proverbs 15:27 He who is _____ for gain troubles his own _____, but he who hates _____ will live.

Luke 12:15 And He said to them, "Take heed and beware of _____, for one's life does not consist in the_____ of the things he _____."

➤ Dictionary.com defines covetousness as *"eager or excessive desire, especially for wealth or possessions."* One of The Ten Commandments explicitly forbids covetousness, and James tells us that it leads to quarrels and death. He reminds us that we need to ask God for the things we need.

Deuteronomy 5:21 You shall not _____your neighbor's wife; and you shall not _____ your neighbor's house, his field, his male servant, his female servant, his ox, his donkey, or _____ that is your neighbor's.

James 4:2 You _____ but do not have. You murder and _____ and cannot _____. You fight and war. Yet you do not have because you do not _____.

➤ **Ignorance** is often mistakenly interpreted as stupidity or lack of wisdom. However, ignorance is a lack of knowledge or information. For our purposes, *ignorance is not knowing or calculating the actual cost of owning an item and not knowing how to manage and adequately account for your money.*

Problems that arise from ignorance include:

• **Buying things you cannot afford because you have not adequately considered the total price.** Everything you own has a cost of ownership above the actual price that you paid for it. Possessions must be maintained, stored, cleaned, and repaired. Some assets, such as vehicles, must also be licensed and are subject to personal property taxes. A car's total cost will include licensing and registration, fuel, insurance, annual inspections, regular maintenance, repairs, and property tax. If you purchase a boat and cannot keep it on your property, you may incur hefty storage and dock fees.

- **Another problem is the failure to balance your checking account and check for bank errors.** If you have ever written a bad check, you know the cost of that mistake. Typically, you will be charged a fee by your bank and the merchant to whom you wrote the check. Often those charges will cause more checks to bounce, leading to more expenses.

➤ **Indulgence** *is buying something that you do not truly need and that has little value to you.* An indulgence purchase is often an impulse purchase—I see an item that I just have to have, and I buy it with little thought about whether I need it or can afford it. Once I get the item home, I may realize that I have no real use for it. An indulgence purchase may also be an item bought to "keep up with the Joneses." Indulgence purchases frequently are relegated to a closet or the garage and collect dust until they are donated to Goodwill or sold for pennies on the dollar in a garage sale.

To avoid indulgence purchases:

- Assess whether you truly need the item desired
- Determine that you have the money to pay for the item
- Take time to research the best price
- Pray about whether or not to make the purchase

The amount of time you spend on the steps above should be proportional to the object's price. For instance, you might decide to buy a new pair of pants in a few minutes, whereas you should take several weeks or perhaps a few months to make a decision about purchasing a new car.

James 5:1, 5 Come now, you rich, weep and howl for your _____ that are coming upon you....You have lived on earth in _____ and luxury.

➤ **Impatience** *is the overwhelming desire to have what I want right now and to refuse to wait.* Impatience frequently arises from a restless desire for change and excitement. It manifests itself in making impulse purchases. To avoid unwise impulse purchases, be sure to go through the above steps.

Schemes that promote a quick path to riches are also a trap for those who are impatient. The Internet abounds with opportunities for people to "get rich" in a short period of time. When considering these ploys, it is best to remember that it is probably not genuine if it sounds too good to be true.

The Bible warns against trying to get rich quickly.

Proverbs 28:22 A man with an _____ eye hastens after _____, and does not consider that _____ will come upon him.

Think About: Which of these attitude problems do the Smiths exhibit?

_____

_____

_____

_____

Let's look at how attitude problems have contributed to the Smith's monetary decisions. The fact that their credit card balances are rising indicates that Jason and MaryAnn are guilty of impatience. They need to delay purchases until they have saved up the money to pay for them. Both of their attitudes regarding discretionary purchases indicate that they believe that the other is guilty of indulgence and, perhaps, greed. MaryAnn's work may require her to be well-dressed in business suits, so she truly needs the clothing; however, it is also likely that she could find good quality clothing without paying for the designer labels. Jason may feel that the electronics he purchases are his reward for working hard and help him to relax. However, he needs to ensure that his purchases (1) fit into his discretionary allowance, (2) are items he truly wants and will use, and (3) are not just being bought to keep up with his friends.

Life Application:

1 Timothy 6:17 *"Command those who are rich in this present age not to be haughty, nor to trust in uncertain riches but in the living God, who gives us richly all things to enjoy."*

Budgeting and saving are essential aspects of managing our money. However, our hope and security cannot be in the size of our bank account. Our hope must indeed be in God. God wants to supply all of our needs, and He wants us to enjoy that which He provides.

Activity: Like Jason and Mary Ann, you cannot effectively create a budget until you know where your money is going. Review your bank statements, credit card bills, utility bills, and other expenses for the past 6 – 12 months to determine how you are currently spending your money. Enter the amounts into the budget worksheet. You may use annual totals or monthly averages. Most people find it is easier to think in terms of monthly averages. We will review your budget and make adjustments in the next lesson.

_____ Family Budget

Income	Monthly Amount
Income	
Less: Tithe	

Spendable Income   _____

Expenses	Monthly Amount
Mortgage or rent	
Gas, Electric, Water	
Cable TV, Internet, phone, cell phone	
Insurance	
Property taxes	
House maintenance	
HOA dues	
Trash	

Total housing expenses _____

Fuel	
Insurance	
Car payment	
Car taxes and registration	
Car maintenance and repairs	

Total car expenses _____

Groceries	
Dining Out	

Total food expenses _____

Clothing	
Debt repayment	
Entertainment/recreation	
Life Insurance	
Medical	
Savings	
Miscellaneous	

Total other expenses _____

Total expenses _____

Total income _____

Excess (shortage) _____

Note:

[1] Larry Burkett, *Family Budget That Work,* Tyndale House Publishers, Inc., 1988.

LESSON 8

Applying Budgeting Principles

In this lesson, we will apply the budgeting principles we learned in Lesson 7. Budgeting principles will never help you accomplish your financial goals until you begin to apply them. God expects us to use wisely the financial resources He provides us. When we demonstrate an ability to do that, God can entrust us with more.

Many people are afraid of budgeting. Other people believe that budgeting does not work for them—they tried it in the past and failed. Budgets typically fail for one of two reasons:

1) We make budgets but fail to follow them
2) We make unrealistic budgets.

Budgeting Involves:
1) Assessing the current situation
2) Setting goals
3) Making a realistic plan to achieve those goals

At the end of Lesson 7, you assessed your current situation by identifying how you spend your income each month. That exercise should have provided you with some insight into whether you live within your means or are accruing debt. In this lesson, we will talk about applying budgeting principles and

SUSAN E. BALL

setting financial goals. In Lesson 9, you will create a budgeting plan to allow you to reach your financial goals. However, before we do that, we first need to take a more in-depth look at income and tithing.

Pay Tithes First

The Bible instructs us to give back a tithe, or ten percent, of our income to the work of the Lord. There is significant debate among Christians about whether they should tithe on gross income or net income. Gross income is the amount your employer has agreed to pay you, and net income is the amount you take home. Your net income is generally significantly less than your gross income because money has been withheld from your check to pay various taxes. The money withheld for taxes is not within your control, nor can you control how the government will spend that money.

Proverbs 3:9 – 10 tell us, *"Honor the Lord with your possessions, And with the firstfruits of all your increase; So your barns will be filled with plenty, And your vats will overflow with new wine."*

My personal belief is that this verse instructs us to pay God first; therefore, I base my tithe on the gross amount of my salary. However, I know people who believe that money we have no control over is not truly ours and does not constitute an increase; these people subtract the amount of taxes withheld and then pay their tithe. I urge you to pray thoughtfully about this and let the Holy Spirit guide you in making this decision for yourself. If you do not pay tithe on taxes withheld, you should tithe on any tax refunds received.

In addition to taxes withheld, you may have money taken out of your check and deposited directly into savings and retirement accounts or used to pay health insurance premiums. You have some control over these funds and discretion regarding how they are spent, so they constitute income, and you should tithe on these sums.

There are other nuances of income and tithing that we could address and that people debate. However, the primary consideration is having the right attitude toward God and toward tithing. 2 Corinthians 9:7 says, *"So let each one give as he purposes in his heart, not grudgingly or of necessity; for God loves a cheerful giver."*

Budgeting Principles that Work

I adapted the information below from Larry Burkett's book *"Family Budgets That Work."*[1]

1) Use a written plan. A written plan helps keep you on track and provides a reference for you. Adjust your budget as your income and/or expenses change. If you are married, your spouse needs to be involved in making the plan.

2) Stick to your plans diligently. Make a plan you can live with and follow it.

3) Provide for God's work from the first part of your income. God enables us to work and provide for our families. All our income truly belongs to God. He asks for only a small portion of it back.

4) Include periodic bills (quarterly insurance premiums, annual HOA fees, etc.) in your budget. Set aside a fixed amount each month to have the money available when it is time to pay these irregularly occurring bills.

5) Set aside amounts to replace furniture, appliances, and fixtures that wear out over time and replace automobiles. I recommend having a separate long-term savings account for these infrequent, large ticket purchases.

6) Set aside money for family vacations and recreation. If possible, budget 5 to 6 percent of your income for recreation and leisure. If you don't have room in your budget for an expensive vacation, consider inexpensive camping and stay-cation options.

7) Save regularly, even if it is only a small amount. Setting aside even $10 or $20 per paycheck gets you in the habit of saving. Increase savings as your budget allows until you can save 5 percent of your income.

8) Control impulse spending. Make a rule to wait at least 24 hours before buying items that were not on your list. Often the desire to purchase the item will go away once you have left the store. If

you decide you really want and/or need the item, buy it only if (1) it fits into your budget, and (2) you have the money to pay for it.

9) Limit your use of credit. Avoid using credit cards to purchase items you cannot afford. Use credit only for large-ticket items that fit into your budget.

10) Plan for gift-giving. Set aside money each month for Christmas and birthday gifts.

11) Watch miscellaneous spending. Miscellaneous spending is a problem area for most families. Track all your cash spending for a month to determine your problem areas and then make a plan to deal with them.

12) Get out of debt. Pay off the smallest debts or debts with the highest interest first while making the minimum payment on all debts. Once you pay off the targeted debt, apply that money to paying off the next debt.

13) Commit to using at least 50 percent of any "windfalls" to paying off debt. Use the remainder of any windfalls to meet shortages in other areas, including clothing and leisure.

Tips for Making Your Budget Work

1) Balance your checkbook every month or more often. Use duplicate checks if possible.

2) Have only one bookkeeper in the family. This should be whichever spouse is better at record-keeping and money management.

3) Develop a sound system for keeping records. Some people put the budgeted amount of cash in an envelope at the beginning of the month and spend only the envelope's money. Other people use Quickbooks, an Excel spreadsheet, or a phone app to track spending. Choose the system that will work best for you.

4) Set family goals. If your children are old enough, include them in your budget discussions. You will be starting them on the road to good financial management, and they will better understand why you cannot always buy them the things they want. Goals should include:

   a. Trust in God to supply your needs

   b. Save money regularly

    c. Family sharing time
    d. Husband and wife time
    e. Ministry to other people
5) Seek good counsel if you have a question, preferably from a Christian financial counselor. Crown Ministries (Crown.org) provides many resources to assist you in budgeting.

Think About:

Why do you think most people do not create and use a family budget to manage their household income?

_____

_____

_____

Are you spending your money in accordance with these principles?

_____

What adjustments should you make to get your expenses more in line with these principles?

_____

_____

_____

If you have not been budgeting, what might motivate you to begin budgeting?

_____

_____

Activity: Make a list of the top financial goals you would like to achieve. These might include: savings to send your children to college, financial independence, early retirement, or to provide for elderly parents.

_____

_____

_____

_____

_____

Life Application

Luke 16:12 _"And if you have not been faithful in what is another man's, who will give you what is your own?"_

As we honor God with our money by being faithful to use it wisely and for His glory, He will be able to trust us with more money and enable us to bless more people and organizations. Budgeting enables us to provide for our family's needs and provide for the work of God's kingdom.

As you continue through the remaining lessons, diligently pray that God will help you to set financial goals that line up with His plans for your life. Ask Him to help you develop a budget that will allow you to achieve your goals and honor Him with your money.

Note:

[1] Larry Burkett, _Family Budget That Work,_ Tyndale House Publishers, Inc., 1988.

LESSON 9

Creating Your Budget

By now, you should have a good grasp of how much money is coming in and going out each month, and you should have set some financial goals. In this lesson, we analyze how to make changes to your monthly spending to balance your budget and work toward achieving your goals.

Housing-related expenses should account for the most sizeable portion of your budget. According to the majority of experts, those expenses should consume no more than 36 percent of your budget. Housing-related costs include your mortgage payment or rent, homeowner's or renter's insurance, utilities, property taxes, and communication expenses for telephone, Internet, and cable television.

Food and auto expenses are the next largest categories of spending. They should account for about 12 percent of your budget. Food expenses include groceries and eating out; be sure to add coffee purchases and snacks. Auto expenses include car payments, fuel, insurance, licenses and taxes, maintenance, and repairs.

After paying for housing, food, and auto expenses, you should have about 40 percent of your budget remaining. Clothing, medical expenses, entertainment, life insurance, savings, and debt reduction will each take about 5 percent, leaving 10 percent for miscellaneous expenses.

Expense Category	Percentage	Includes
Housing	36	Mortgage or rent, utilities, cable/phone, insurance, property tax, maintenance, HOA dues, trash
Food	12	Groceries, dining out, ice cream truck, coffee shop, vending machines
Auto	12	Fuel, insurance, payment, taxes, repairs
Clothing	5	
Medical	5	Prescriptions, co-pays, insurance (not taken out of check)
Entertainment	5	Movies, books, recreation
Life insurance	5	
Savings	5	
Debt reduction	5	Payments above current month's charges
Miscellaneous	10	Gifts, haircuts, school and office supplies, magazines
Total	100	

Sample "ideal" budgets based on these percentages are shown below for Spendable Incomes ranging from $2,500 to $6,000. We define Spendable Income as take-home income minus tithe. Someone whose spendable income is $2,500 has a budget of only $900 per month for all housing-related expenses. Obviously, that is not feasible in many areas of the country. A person in that salary range will have to allocate more money to housing and less to other expense categories. Living within one's means can be challenging and often requires making sacrifices.

Sample "Ideal" Budgets

Spendable Income:

$2,5000 $3,000 $3,500 $4,000 $4,5000 $5,000 $5,500 $,6000

Expenses

Housing (36%)	$900	$1,080	$1,260	$1,440	$1,620	$1,800	$1,960	$2,160
Food (12%)	$300	$360	$420	$480	$540	$600	$660	$720
Car (12%)	$300	$360	$420	$480	$540	$600	$660	$720

Other								
Debt pymt (5%)	$125	$150	$175	$200	$225	$250	$275	$300
Clothing (5%)	$125	$150	$175	$200	$225	$250	$275	$300
Savings (5%)	$125	$150	$175	$200	$225	$250	$275	$300
Medical (5%)	$125	$150	$175	$200	$225	$250	$275	$300
Fun (5%)	$125	$150	$175	$200	$225	$250	$275	$300
Life Ins. (5%)	$125	$150	$175	$200	$225	$250	$275	$300
Misc. (10%)	$250	$300	$350	$400	$450	$500	$550	$600

Total Expenses:	$2,500	$3,000	$3,500	$4,000	$4,500	$5,000	$5,500	$,6000
Excess (shortage):	$0	$0	$0	$0	$0	$0	$0	$0

Activity:

In Lesson 7, you determined how you were spending your money. Look back on those patterns now. Are you spending more each month than you are earning? We all have occasional months in which expenses exceed income, and we have to (1) take money out of savings to cover the costs or (2) use credit cards or other forms of debt to tide us over. Of course, if this situation is a regular occurrence, you will accumulate debt and dig yourself into a financial hole.

The lower your income, the larger the percentage of it is needed to pay for necessary expenses. You must have a place to live, food, and transportation. The other categories are somewhat discretionary. If the required expenses consume more than the recommended 60 percent of your budget, you must cut back on your discretionary categories.

Case Study:

Lisa and Joey Taylor have three children. Lisa is a full-time homemaker who homeschools the children. Joey is an electrician earning $72,000 per year. After taxes, health insurance, and other deductions, Joey brings home $4,800 per month. Joey and Lisa rent a three-bedroom house for $1,400 per month. Renter's insurance, utilities, telephone, cable, and trash service bring their total monthly household expenses to $1,910 per month.

Joey's employer provides him with a work vehicle. He is allowed to drive it home so that the family can get by with one car. The Taylors bought a gently-used minivan 3 years ago. They have 12 remaining car payments of $218. Their monthly costs associated with the vehicle are $140 for gas, $72 for insurance, and $10 for license and registration. Additionally, they budget $50 per month for annual maintenance and repairs. Since their car is relatively new, they have had few repair bills and have saved up an emergency repair fund of $975.

Lisa keeps the family grocery bills down by using coupons, stocking up on staples when they are on sale, and growing many of their vegetables. She studies the grocery ads and plans meals using meats that are on sale. She enjoys cooking and makes most meals from scratch. Thus, Lisa can keep grocery purchases at an average of $275 per month. The family orders pizza twice a month on payday Friday nights at the cost of $22 and goes out to lunch on Sundays after church, spending an average of $45. Joey packs a lunch 4 days a week and eats out once a week; lunch out typically costs Joey $8. Joey and Lisa have a date night once a month; they usually splurge on a nice dinner at a casual restaurant at the cost of about $40.

Think About: Without doing any calculations, how do you think the Taylors are doing regarding spending in the three basic categories: housing, auto, and food?

_____

_____

_____

_____

The Taylors seem to be doing many things right and to be in pretty good financial shape. We must do some calculations, however, to get a clear picture of their financial situation. You can see the Taylor's current spending in the three basic expense categories in the table below.

Taylor Family Budget—Basic Expenses

Income	Monthly Amount
Income	$4,800
Less: Tithe	480
Spendable Income	$4,320

Expenses	Monthly Amount
Mortgage or rent	$1,400
Gas, Electric, Water	220
Cable TV, Internet, phone, cell phone	145
Insurance	42
Property taxes	
House maintenance	
HOA dues	
Trash	20
Total housing expenses	$1,910

Fuel	$140
Insurance	72
Car payment	218
Car taxes and registration	10
Car maintenance and repairs	50
Total car expenses	**$490**

Groceries	$275
Dining Out	296
Total food expenses	**$571**

Total expenses for basic expenses	**$2,971**
Optimal budget for basic expenses	$2,592
Overspending on basic expenses	$379

After paying a tithe of 10 percent, Joey and Lisa have $4,320 to spend each month. Their housing expenses of $1,910 are just over 44 percent of their spendable income. Based on an ideal budget, they would need to keep their household expenses at $1,557. Joey and Lisa should examine their expenses to determine if it is possible to cut back on their housing category. It is unlikely to cut out the $353 necessary to bring this expense down to 36 percent. Therefore, Joey and Lisa will need to reduce spending in some other categories below the amounts in an ideal budget.

The ideal budget specifies that 12 percent of spendable income be used for auto and 12 percent for food. Based on their spendable income of $4,320, Joey and Lisa have $518 to spend on auto and $518 to spend on food. Again, they are doing many things right. Their auto expenses of $490 are below the budgeted amount by $28. However, their food expenses total $571, or $53 over the ideal budget amount.

The Taylors do not display any of the wrong attitudes toward budgeting that we looked at in Lesson 7. They are not greedy, indulgent, or impatient. Still, they are spending $379 more for basic expenses than the ideal budget allows.

Think About: Should the Taylors be concerned about their overspending in the three basic categories? What should they do before making any budgeting decisions?

_____

_____

_____

_____

The Taylors will want to examine each of these spending categories to determine if they can make some cuts. Before making any big decisions, such as selling their vehicle or banning all dining out, they need to look at the other spending categories. It may be that their spending in other categories makes up for the overspending in the basic ones.

Since Lisa is a stay-at-home mother and homeschools the children, the family clothing budget is relatively modest. Lisa and the children each have a few nice outfits that they wear to church and on special occasions; however, most of their clothing is casual. Joey's work uniform is khaki work pants or blue jeans with a company-issued shirt. Therefore, he also only needs casual clothes and a few suits. Lisa shops for bargains and can clothe her family for an average of $100 per month, which is well below the ideal budget's $216 clothing allowance.

Health insurance premiums are deducted from Joey's paycheck and are not included in the budget. Joey and Lisa are both healthy and take no regular medications. Each year, their only expected medical expenses are regular checkups and the occasional sick visit, so their medical expenses average $50 each month. The ideal budget allows for $216 in medical costs.

The budget also allows for $216 to be put toward debt reduction. Lisa and Joey have no debt other than their car payment, and they can allocate the $216 to other expenses.

In these three categories, the Taylors are $498 below the ideal budget. Thus, we find that underspending in these areas has more than offset overspending in the other three. The other categories of spending—entertainment and recreation, insurance, savings, and miscellaneous—allow for more discretion in spending than the other areas. Based on the ideal budget guidelines, the Taylors have $1,080 to be spent in these categories, and they also have $118 that has been saved from other areas.

The Taylor family illustrates how overspending in one category can be offset by underspending in another. The Taylors are providing for their family while living within their means, which allows them to live debt-free, except for their car payment, and with little financial stress.

Taylor Family Budget—Basic and Discretionary Expenses

Income	Monthly Amount
Income	$4,800
Less: Tithe	480
Spendable Income	$4,320

Expenses	Monthly Amount
Total housing expenses	$1,910

Total car expenses	$490

Total food expenses	$571

Clothing	$100
Debt repayment	0
Entertainment/recreation	150
Life Insurance	80
Medical	50
Savings	216
Miscellaneous	350

Total other expenses		$946

Total expenses		$3,917
Total income		$4,320
Excess (shortage)		$403

Activity: Review your expense categories. In what areas are you exceeding the recommended budget percentages? In what areas are you spending less?

_____

_____

_____

_____

If your expenses exceed your income, you MUST make changes. You want your expenditures below your income level. What immediate changes can you make to your spending habits?

_____

_____

_____

_____

Setting Goals

Setting financial goals is an essential part of the budgeting process. Setting goals helps you stick to your budget. It is not fun to track expenses and deny yourself the things you want. It becomes more comfortable when you know that this effort is helping you to achieve your goals. Your goals can be short-term and easily achievable, such as saving money for a weekend trip, or longer-term, such as saving for a new car or a down payment on a house.

In the late 1990s, my husband and I had a goal of buying a pizza franchise. We realized that we would need a significant amount of cash to put into the restaurant and that we would have to cut back our living expenses when my husband left his salaried job since we would be working for ourselves. We spent a year researching the business and possible locations. During that time, we stopped going out to eat and bought only items that were absolute necessities. We knew we would be moving to a different state and sold the furniture that would not make the move. When it came time to move, we downsized from a 2,200 square foot home with an in-ground pool on two acres to a 1,700 square foot townhouse. The smaller home reduced our mortgage payment as well as our utility costs. We made sacrifices willingly to enable us to achieve our goal.

You must set financial goals for yourself. If you are married, involve your spouse in making budget decisions. You need to set goals that are realistic and achievable.

Activity:

> ➤ Review the financial goals you listed at the end of Lesson 8. Do you believe each of these goals is realistic and achievable?

_____

_____

> ➤ If these goals are not realistic and achievable, how might you adjust them?

_____

_____

Case Study:

Lisa and Joey would like to buy a home of their own. They know that they can afford to buy a home if they can keep the total monthly payment—principal and interest, property taxes, and homeowners' insurance—equal to or less than their current rent payment of $1,400 per month. After speaking with a lender, they learn that they can qualify for a loan of $200,000 if they can save up a $10,000 down payment. At present, they have $1,236 in a savings account earmarked for unexpected expenses, $3,200 in a long-term savings account, and $975 in an account for future car repairs.

Think About: What changes would you advise the Taylors to make to save up the $10,000 in as short a time as possible?

_____

_____

_____

_____

Joey and Lisa might be tempted to use the car repair fund toward the down payment on a house; however, that would be risky. They need to maintain some funds for car repairs or other household emergencies that might arise. Since they have a significant balance in that account, they can decide not to put any more money in that account until the balance falls below $500. This step would free up $50 per month to go into savings.

The ideal budget directs them to save 5 percent, or $216, each month. Joey and Lisa use this money for emergencies and unexpected expenses. They will continue this practice and will not use this money toward the down payment.

When Joey and Lisa examined their entertainment and recreation, life insurance, and miscellaneous expenditures over the past year, they found that they spent an average of $150 per month on entertainment and recreation, $80 per month on life insurance, and $350 on miscellaneous expenses.

Joey felt it would be unwise to reduce his life insurance premiums. However, he and Lisa agreed that they could shave $50 per month off both the entertainment and recreation budget and the miscellaneous budget. They also decided to forego two Sunday lunches per month, saving $90 per month. They discussed their decisions with their children and received their support.

From their budget worksheet above, we can see that they currently have an excess of $403 per month, going into a long-term savings account. This money will go toward the down payment on the house.

Below is the Taylor's revised budget. With the changes, they can save $643 per month. They have $3,200 in savings currently, so they need $6,800 to reach their goal of $10,000 for a down payment. If they are faithful to the new budget, they will reach their goal in eleven months. In less than a year, they should be able to move into a home of their own. While they are saving money for their home purchase, the Taylors can research the market to decide on their preferred neighborhoods and to get a realistic idea of the size and condition of a house they can purchase on their budget.

Taylor Family Budget—Revised to Save for House Down Payment

Income	Monthly Amount
Income	$4,800
Less: Tithe	480
Spendable Income	$4,320

Expenses	Monthly Amount
Mortgage or rent	$1,400
Gas, Electric, Water	220
Cable TV, Internet, phone	145

Insurance	42
Property taxes	
Cell phone	83
House maintenance	
HOA dues	
Trash	20
Total housing expenses	$1,910

Fuel	$140
Insurance	72
Car payment	218
Car taxes and registration	10
Car maintenance and repairs	
Total car expenses	$440

Groceries	$275
Dining Out	206
Total food expenses	$481

Clothing	$100
Debt repayment	0
Entertainment/recreation	100
Life Insurance	80
Medical	50
Savings	216
Miscellaneous	300
Total other expenses	$846

Total expenses	$3,677
Total income	$4,320
Excess (shortage)	$643

With patience and self-control, the Taylor family can own a home in a relatively short time. They will be able to purchase a home they can afford and will have a large enough down payment to have immediate equity in their home.

Many young homeowners today get into problems with their mortgages due to:

1) Impatience—they rush into buying a home without saving up an adequate down payment and without determining the mortgage payment they can afford,
2) Ignorance—they do not count the actual costs of owning a home and therefore buy a house which is more expensive than they can afford,
3) Indulgence—they want to buy a home with lots of upgrades, such as granite counter-tops, stainless steel appliances, and large master bathrooms.

Joey and Lisa will avoid the attitude problems listed above by carefully determining what they can afford to pay for a house, faithfully sticking to the budget they have created, and praying for God's direction in their house purchase.

Activity: Like Joey and Lisa, you will need to make some sacrifices to achieve your financial goals. Review your budget and consider what areas you can reduce your spending to achieve your goals. List those areas below.

_____

_____

_____

_____

Activity:

Using the budget worksheet below, make adjustments to your budget to reflect the sacrifices you will make to achieve your financial goals. What goal will you focus on reaching first? Based on the changes you have made to your budget, how soon will you reach that goal?

_____

_____

_____

_____

_____ **Family Budget--Revised**

Income	Monthly Amount
Income	
Less: Tithe	

Spendable Income _____

Expenses	Monthly Amount
Mortgage or rent	
Gas, Electric, Water	
Cable TV, Internet, phone, cell phone	
Insurance	
Property taxes	
House maintenance	
HOA dues	
Trash	

Total housing expenses _____

Fuel	
Insurance	
Car payment	
Car taxes and registration	
Car maintenance and repairs	

Total car expenses _____

Groceries	
Dining Out	

Total food expenses _____

Clothing	
Debt repayment	
Entertainment/recreation	
Life Insurance	
Medical	
Savings	
Miscellaneous	

Total other expenses _____

Total expenses _____

Total income _____

Excess (shortage) _____

LESSON 10

Dealing with Debt

This lesson will explore steps to pay off debts and ensure that debt does not entrap you. God's word tells us not to be in debt. When we spend money beyond what we have earned, we go into debt. In some cases, we cannot avoid debt, so we must determine that we will repay the debt entirely in a timely manner.

Many people across our nation are burdened with a staggering amount of debt and struggle to maintain their current lifestyles. The 2019 Consumer Financial Literary Survey found that 40 percent of Americans cannot pay off their credit cards each month.[1] If you are one of those people, I hope these guidelines will enable you to become financially free of this debt.

Think About: How does mortgage debt differ from consumer debt and credit card debt?

_____

_____

_____

_____

A **mortgage** is a loan used to purchase a home. The home provides collateral for the loan and will retain its value for many decades if properly maintained. It may even increase in value and provide equity to the owner when it is sold.

A **consumer loan** is a debt that is used to purchase items with a much shorter life span. Consumer loans are taken out for purchases of automobiles, furniture, and appliances. These items should last for several years; however, they do not retain their value. If you would need to sell them before the end of their useful life, you would most likely get only a fraction of the price you paid for them.

Credit card purchases are often used to buy consumables—items that are used up in a short time. Consumables include food, gasoline, clothing, and recreation. Even if you pay your credit card bill in full each month, you will likely consume the purchases before paying the bill.

Student loans are another significant source of debt. The student counts on the fact that the education will open doors to a higher paying job. However, one needs to be careful that the school loan cost does not outweigh the benefit of the degree or certification earned.

Think About: Is it wrong for a Christian to use debt to buy things she needs?

_____

_____

_____

_____

Generally speaking, a Christian should avoid debt as much as possible. Proverbs 22:7 tells us that debt leads to bondage. *"The rich rules over the poor, and the borrower is servant to the lender."* God does not want His people to be in bondage.

What about mortgage debt? Indeed, a mortgage represents money that you owe. However, a home purchase is viewed as an investment. Very few of us would ever be able to own a home if taking out a mortgage was not an option. When taking out a mortgage, pray about the purchase very carefully and be sure to purchase a home that you can afford on your current income.

There will be times that you may need to borrow money for a significant purchase that you cannot delay. Ideally, you will begin setting aside some money each month to pay cash for such purchases. Automobiles and appliances need to be replaced periodically; saving for those future purchases should be part of your budget.

If you are committed to paying off your credit card balance in full each month, you can benefit financially from using credit cards. However, for many people, any benefits are outweighed by the risks. Credit cards pose a real financial threat when they are not used wisely, and spending is not kept within budget limits. Studies have shown that people are likely to spend 20 percent more when paying by credit card than when paying by cash. You should not use credit cards unless you are committed to paying the balances off each month.

Many young adults struggle under the weight of enormous student loans. A college degree or vocational school certification can enhance job opportunities and lead to a higher salary. However, a student should weigh all options available for furthering her education. Consider attending a local college or university or a community college, if there is one in your area. Today there are many online degrees and certification programs available. These options can provide training that is desired at very affordable rates.

If you are currently in debt, the following steps will help you plan to get out of debt and stay out of debt.

Steps to Getting Out of Debt

1) Determine in your heart to repay all your debts, as the Lord enables you.
   Psalm 37:21, "*The wicked borrows and does not repay, but the righteous shows mercy and gives.*"

2) Establish a payment schedule that includes all creditors.
   a) Make a list of all debts from smallest to largest or from the highest interest rate to lowest.
   b) Determine first to pay off either (1) the smallest debt or (2) the debt with the highest interest rate.
   c) Make minimum payments on all debts except the one to be paid off first.
   d) Allocate as much money as possible each month to paying off the debt being retired first.
   e) When one debt is paid in full, concentrate efforts on the next debt.

3) Contact creditors and ask for a lower interest rate. They are more likely to do this if you have been faithfully making at least minimum payments each month. If this doesn't work, research other options, such as using a lower-rate credit card to pay off a high-interest rate balance.

4) Contact all creditors, honestly relate your problems, and arrange an equitable repayment plan.

5) Buy on a cash basis, and sacrifice your wants and desires until you are current. Allow God to meet your needs without taking on more debt.

Psalm 37:7 *"Rest in the Lord, and wait patiently for Him."*

6) Consider taking out a home equity loan or secured personal loan to pay off credit card debt. Credit card companies charge interest rates of up to 24 percent or more. If you own your car or you have equity in your home, you may be able to borrow at a much lower rate, in the range of 4 – 9 percent. This could save you a great deal of money in interest payments. However, it is crucial to note that this process only works if you begin to live within your budget. People who fail to live within their budgets quickly wind up with more credit card debt, in addition to the home equity loan or personal loan.

7) Consider selling assets of value to reduce your debt. You may have a boat or motorcycle used purely for recreational purposes or other assets of value that are not necessities. Selling these items could allow you to pay off some loans and relieve stress in your budget and life.

8) Make hard choices. I once counseled a woman who needed extensive dental work. She and her husband were both retired and lived on a fixed income. After reviewing their budget, they decided that the only way to pay for the dental work was to use the $100 a month they had budgeted for gifts. This was not an easy decision, but it was the correct one for them. They found a dentist who agreed to do the work for twelve payments of $100. They explained to their children and grandchildren that they would not be purchasing any gifts for one year. Their family members were incredibly supportive. You may find that you need to give up something for a while to pay off your debt.

9) Do not cosign for another person unless you are able and willing to pay off the debt if he/she cannot do so.

Proverbs 22:26 – 27 *"Do not be one of those who shakes hands in a pledge, one of those who is surety for debts; if you have nothing with which to pay, why should he take away your bed from under you?"*

10) Do not count on future raises to pay for today's expenses.

James 4:13 – 15, *"Come now, you who say, 'Today or tomorrow we will go to such and such city, spend a year there, buy and sell, and make a profit;' whereas you do not know what will happen tomorrow. For what is your life? It is even a vapor that appears for a little time and then vanishes away. Instead, you ought to say, 'If the Lord wills, we shall live and do this or that.'"*

If you are dealing with overwhelming debt, you may need to seek assistance from a debt counselor. Also, seek help from the One who supplies all our needs. God wants to help you and is waiting for you to bring your burdens to Him. Psalm 55:22, *"Cast your burden on the Lord, and He shall sustain you; He shall never permit the righteous to be moved."*

Case Study:

Janet and Harry have been living beyond their means for several years and have built up quite a bit of debt. After studying the principles presented in *Honoring God with Your Money,* they have committed to getting out of debt as soon as possible. They begin the process by listing their debts from smallest to largest. Their debts are:

Creditor	Total Owed	Current Monthly Payment
Best Buy	$375	$25
Target	$550	$30
Visa	$795	$40
Mastercard	$1,400	$65
Bank Loan	$2,500	$80
Car Loan	$12,500	$400

Janet and Harry have worked together to develop a budget. By cutting back on nonessentials, they can continue making the current payments on their debt and an additional payment toward $50 each month. They have also committed to not charging anything else until they are debt-free. They decide to apply the $50 extra payment to paying off the smallest debt first. Therefore, they increase the payment to Best Buy to $75. This step will allow them to pay off the Best Buy debt in 5 months.

At the end of the 5 months, their other balances have also decreased. We will ignore interest that will accrue and reduce each balance by 5 payments for simplicity's sake. Their new debt totals will be:

Creditor	Total Owed	Current Monthly Payment
Target	$400	$30
Visa	$595	$40
Mastercard	$1,075	$65
Bank Loan	$2,100	$80
Car Loan	$10,500	$400

They increase the Target payment to $105 ($30 + $75). This allows them to pay off the Target card in 4 months, and their new debt totals fall to:

Creditor	Total Owed	Current Monthly Payment
Visa	$435	$40
Mastercard	$815	$65
Bank Loan	$1,780	$80
Car Loan	$8,900	$400

They continue the pattern, increasing the Visa payment to $145. It will take them three months to pay off the Visa bill. Their remaining balances will be $620 on Mastercard, $1,540 on the bank loan, and $7,700 on the car loan.

They will have paid off three of their six debts in one year and will have reduced their total debt from $18,075 to $9,860. If they continue in this manner, Harry and Janet will have paid off all their debts except for the car loan in another seven months. It will take an additional seven months to pay off the car loan.

Altogether it will take Janet and Harry a little more than two years to pay off the debt they have accumulated. That sounds like a long time, yet it is a very reachable goal. They will have to exercise discipline and self-control to achieve their dream of paying off their debts. In reality, interest would accrue on all these debts during the repayment period, so it would take a bit longer to pay them off.

Harry and Janet's situation is not unlike that of many Americans today. Whether due to job layoffs, illnesses, misfortunes, or poor money management, many Americans have numerous consumer loan accounts and feel that they are drowning in debt. However, this example illustrates that it is possible with commitment and dedication to become debt-free.

Activity: Make a list of all your credit cards and consumer debt. Arrange the list according to the smallest debt to the largest debt.

_____

_____

_____

_____

_____

_____

_____

_____

Beside each debt, write the amount that you pay each month. Hopefully, you are paying more than the minimum, but don't fret if you are only paying the minimum. Now calculate how quickly you can pay off the smallest debt if you can increase your payment by $50 per month.

Examine your budget and prayerfully consider how you can cut back your other expenses by $50 per month. Commit to making these changes and paying off the smallest debt. When the smallest debt is paid off, move on to the next smallest debt, and so forth.

Some financial advisors counsel clients to pay off the debt with the highest interest rate first. Over the long run, that policy will save some money in interest fees. However, my experience has been that clients need to have the psychological encouragement of paying off debts. By starting with the smallest debt, you pay off a balance in the shortest time, and that achievement provides motivation to stick with the plan.

Example of Poor Credit Card Use

Credit card companies make money (1) on transaction fees when you charge a purchase and (2) on interest and late fees on accumulated balances. Many companies set the minimum balance so low that it could take as long as 6 - 9 years to pay off the debt if you did not charge anything else on that account. The interest that would accumulate during this time adds significantly to the cost of the item purchased.

The following example is based on a close friend's true experience. I will call him John Doe. John purchased a riding lawn mower for $3,600 from a well-known retail chain. He charged the mower on a store card at an interest rate of 21 percent. The minimum monthly payment of $98 was calculated, and the loan would be repaid in 5 years. If John made only the minimum payment and made all the payments on time, the mower's total costs would have been $98 * 60 = $5,880. The total interest paid would have been $2,216, which is more than 60 percent of the original purchase price.

When I met with John, he had been paying on the mower for 24 months. His payment record looked like this:

Month	Payment	Interest	Late Fee	Balance
1	$98.00	$63.00	$30.00	$3,595.00
2	$98.00	$62.91	$30.00	$3,589.91
3	$98.00	$62.82	$30.00	$3,584.94
4	$98.00	$62.73	$30.00	$3,579.47
5	$196.00	$62.64		$3,446.11
6	$98.00	$60.31		$3,408.42
7	$98.00	$59.65		$3,370.06

8	$98.00	$58.98		$3,331.04
9	$98.00	$58.29		$3,291.33
10	$98.00	$57.60		$3,250.93
11	$98.00	$56.89		$3,209.82
12	$98.00	$56.17	$30.00	$3,179.99
13	$98.00	$55.96		$3,155.96
14	$98.00	$55.23	$30.00	$3,143.19
15	$98.00	$55.01		$3,100.19
16		$54.25	$30.00	$3,184.45
17	$98.00	$55.73	$30.00	$3,172.18
18	$196.00	$55.51		$3,031.69
19	$98.00	$53.05		$2,986.74
20	$98.00	$52.27		$2,941.01
21	$98.00	$51.47		$2,894.48
22	$98.00	$50.65		$2,847.13
23	$98.00	$49.82		$2,798.96
24	$98.00	$48.98		$2,749.94

Because of a misunderstanding about the first payment date on the card, John's first four payments were considered late. Eventually, he reviewed his bill and made a catch-up payment in month 5. He made the next seven payments on time, but he made several more payments late before getting back on track. At this point, John had been assessed $240 in late fees and increased his expected accumulated interest on the loan by $145. The lawn mower's total expected cost was now $6,265, which was 74 percent more than the original purchase price.

Ironically, at this time, John had some money in savings. We determined that he could use his savings to make an additional payment of $1,000. This payment reduced his expected interest on the loan by $659, making the lawn mower's total cost $5,606. After making the additional payment, John called the credit card company and asked them to reduce his interest rate. It was lowered from 21 percent to 12 percent, saving even more in interest.

John learned some expensive lessons about credit card debt, including:

1) Make sure you understand the terms of any debt you take on. Ask questions and read the sales agreement carefully. Make sure you know the total costs of the debt and when the first payment is due.
2) Never pay late, and never skip a payment. Interest and late fees will apply and will add significantly to the total costs of the debt. Some companies will increase your interest rate if you have two or more late payments.
3) Make more than the minimum payment whenever you can. If John had simply rounded his payment up to $100, he would have saved $83 in interest and paid off the lawnmower two months earlier. If he had paid an extra $15 per month, he would have saved $503 in interest and cut out 13 months of payment.
4) If you find yourself in over your head, call the credit card company and try to renegotiate the debt.

Car Purchases

I can recall very vividly a conversation I had with a close friend many years ago in which she stated that she always expected to have a car payment. She believed it was normal and expected always to take out a loan to purchase a vehicle. Consequently, she and her husband replaced vehicles more frequently than I was accustomed to, often trading in a 2- to 5-year-old car for a newer model.

This was a new point of view for me. My parents purchased their first car in 1955 and sold it in 1974. We were a one-car family until 1965 when my father bought a brand-new station wagon for cash. I was in first grade at the time. We still had that station wagon when I learned to drive, and I drove it until my junior year of college; we replaced it only when an inattentive driver ran into the back of it. The station wagon was 15 years old at the time of the accident. My father gave the damaged vehicle to a young neighbor; he repaired and repainted it and drove it for several more years.

My husband and I have made a point to purchase gently-used, low mileage cars, and we typically keep them for 8 – 10 years. We have sometimes taken out loans for car purchases, but when we do, it is always with the intent of keeping the car well beyond the point at which the loan is paid off. And, we have always committed to paying off the car loan as quickly as possible. In two cases, we were required to take out a car loan and maintain the loan for at least four months to take advantage of the car manufacturer's price incentives. We calculated that the saving on the purchase price outweighed any interest charges expected, especially as we committed to paying off the car loan at the end of the four-month mandatory period.

When I was a young adult, our pastor issued the following challenge to our congregation:

1) Drive your current car for four years after it is paid off.
2) Put the money that had been going to make the car payment into a dedicated savings account.
3) At the end of the four years, you will have enough money to pay cash for your next car and have enough left over for a trip to Europe.

The pastor took that challenge himself. And sure enough, after four years, he and his wife took a three-week trip to Europe. While there, he purchased a gently-used Mercedes Benz and had it shipped back to the United States. He paid for the trip, the car, and the shipping fees using the money he had saved. He was helped in his endeavor by significantly higher interest rates on savings accounts than we have experienced in recent times. If I were to take his challenge today, I might not save enough for a trip to Europe, but I believe I could undoubtedly save enough to purchase a car for cash.

It will not always be possible to save up the money to pay cash for a car, especially when you are young. However, most of us should continue driving our current vehicles for a few years after they are paid off. If you continue to make your "car payment" to your savings account, you will have a nice sum saved up for a down payment when you do buy a car. A substantial down payment will give you negotiating power and help you get a better deal on a vehicle; the smaller balance financed will yield a smaller monthly car payment.

You can also save money on car purchases by buying gently used cars rather than brand new cars. When we car shop, my husband looks for cars that are 1 – 3 years old with 15,000 – 30,000 miles. We can usually find a vehicle we like for about half the price of a new car. There is an old adage that a new car's value significantly decreases when it is driven off the lot. Let someone else absorb the depreciation and get a great deal on a "newer" used car when they trade up to their next brand-new vehicle.

Activity:

How much is your current car payment? _____

Multiply your car payment by 36. _____

This is the amount you could save by keeping your current vehicle three years after the loan is paid in full.

Multiply your car payment by 48. _____

This is the amount you could save by keeping your current vehicle four years after the loan is paid in full.

I know many people whose car payments exceed $500 per month. If they followed this plan, they could save $18,000 in 3 years and $24,000 in 4 years. Most people should be able to purchase a vehicle that meets their needs for $24,000. It will require patience, self-discipline, and careful shopping, but the reward will certainly be worth the effort.

Note:

[1] 2019 Consumer Financial Literacy Survey, https://www.nfcc.org/data/.

LESSON 11

Savings and Investments

Most financial experts recommend that everyone make a regular habit of saving 5 percent of their income. A goal for savings should be to accumulate enough savings to cover 3 - 6 months of living expenses as a cushion for periods of unemployment due to layoffs and extended illness.

Of course, as Christians, we know that God will supply all our needs. Jesus told His disciples not to worry about the future because God would take care of them. *"Do not worry about your life, what you will eat or what you will drink; nor about your body, what you will put on. Is not life more than food and the body more than clothing? Look at the birds of the air, for they neither sow nor reap nor gather into barns; yet your heavenly Father feeds them. Are you not of more value than they?"* Matthew 6:25 – 26

Jesus was saying that we should put our trust in God. However, He did not suggest that we should be foolish with our money or fail to make provisions for our future. We know that life is filled with good times and bad times. Sometimes we will have more money than we need and at other times we will face financial difficulties. We need to set money aside in the good times to help us through the tough times.

Lesson from the Old Testament: Joseph Prepares for a Famine

There are many lessons to be learned from the story of Joseph in the book of Genesis. For our purposes, we will focus on how God used Joseph to prepare a nation to survive a challenging time that was in its future.

Joseph's story begins in Genesis, chapter 37. His brothers were jealous of him and sold him into slavery. Sometime later, Joseph was called upon to interpret a dream for Pharaoh. We find the interpretation of that dream in Genesis 41: 29 – 36:

> *Indeed seven years of great plenty will come throughout all the land of Egypt; but after them seven years of famine will arise, and all the plenty will be forgotten in the land of Egypt; and the famine will deplete the land. So the plenty will not be known in the land because of the famine following, for it will be very severe. And the dream was repeated to Pharaoh twice because the thing is established by God, and God will shortly bring it to pass.*

> *"Now therefore, let Pharaoh select a discerning and wise man, and set him over the land of Egypt. Let Pharaoh do this, and let him appoint officers over the land, to collect one-fifth of the produce of the land of Egypt in the seven plentiful years. And let them gather all the food of those good years that are coming, and store up grain under the authority of Pharaoh, and let them keep food in the cities. Then that food shall be as a reserve for the land for the seven years of famine which shall be in the land of Egypt, that the land may not perish during the famine."*

Think About:

> ➤ What does this story teach us about savings and being prepared to handle tough times?

_____

_____

> ➤ What would have happened if Pharaoh had not listened to Joseph and made provisions for the famine to come?

_____

_____

God clearly instructed Joseph to counsel Pharaoh to save food in the times of plenty to meet the coming need. God expects us to use wisely the resources that He provides. In times of plenty, we should save and make preparations for future needs. We do not usually have the warning to prepare as the Egyptians did; however, we know that difficult times will come, and we should be prepared. If we don't get ready, our trials will be even more challenging. If Pharaoh had ignored Joseph, many of his countrymen would have died of starvation.

Think About: After Joseph's father died, his brothers feared he would finally retaliate against them for the evil they did to him. In Genesis 50:20 Joseph told them, *"You meant evil against me, but God meant it for good, in order to bring it about as it is this day, to save many people alive."*

➤ How would the future of Joseph's family have been different if Joseph had not been sent ahead of them to Egypt to prepare for the famine?

_____

_____

_____

_____

Joseph was able to fully forgive his brothers because he served the Lord with all his heart. He knew that it was not God's will for his brothers to oppress him. Yet, Joseph could see how God used this difficult situation to bring honor to God, provide for Joseph's family, and reunite Joseph with them. By correctly interpreting the warning God had given Pharaoh and convincing Pharaoh of the need to prepare for tough times, Joseph saved Egypt and his own family.

Activity: Think back on a time of financial hardship that your family faced. Can you recognize ways in which God prepared your family ahead of time to survive the difficult time?

_____

_____

_____

_____

In 2007, I was teaching math in a private Christian school. I felt the Holy Spirit prompting me that it was time to leave that position. Without having a new job lined up, I gave notice that I would not be returning. I had to trust God that I was following His will and that He would reveal His plan to me in His time.

I finished the school year and was hired in the fall to be a business consultant helping people establish and grow small businesses. The job paid more, and I got better health benefits at a lower premium. The net change in income was about $1,000 per month. In the fall of 2008, our area began to feel severe effects of the recession, and, right after Christmas, my husband lost his job. He was unemployed for most of the next three years. His salary had been more than double mine.

Consequently, we lived for those three years on a fraction of what we had been earning. It was tough, but God saw us through and blessed us in many ways. Those three years would have been much harder if I had not listened to God and changed jobs. God knew what was ahead of us, and He led us to take steps to make the situation much more bearable.

Developing a Savings Plan

For those struggling financially and unable to meet current expenses, savings are not an option. Everyone else should make a goal to save at least a small amount out of each paycheck and to increase that amount as circumstances allow. Regular deposits, even tiny ones, into a savings account will, over time, amass interest. Proverbs 13:11 echoes this sentiment, *"Dishonest money dwindles away, but whoever gathers money little by little makes it grow."* (NIV)

Getting into the habit of saving can be difficult, so I offer the following steps to get started on a regular, steady savings plan.

1) Acknowledge that God's word tells us that it is wise to save in the good times for lean times.
   a) **Proverbs 6:6 – 8** *"Go to the ant, you sluggard! Consider her ways and be wise, which, having no captain, overseer or ruler, provides her supplies in the summer and gathers her food in the harvest."*
   b) **Proverbs 21:20** *"There is desirable treasure, and oil in the dwelling of the wise, but a foolish man squanders it."*

2) Develop a system for putting money directly into savings, using one of the following:

a) Use your company's payroll automatic savings deposit, if possible. This puts the money directly into savings before you receive it.

b) Set up an automatic bank transfer from your checking account to your savings account.

c) Write your savings account a check just as if it were a creditor.

3) When an existing debt is cleared, allocate any extra money toward the next largest debt. When all consumer debt is settled, then reallocate that money to savings.

4) Set goals for the items that you desire so that you can see the progress. Having a plan for savings will keep you focused and less likely to fritter money away on things that are not truly needed. This money should be in addition to your long-term savings for emergencies.

5) Use the money-saving tips provided in Appendix A to reduce expenses and free up more money to put into savings.

Investing

If you have created a budget and are following it, you will eventually wind up with more in savings than you need for an emergency fund. At that point, you should think and pray about investing your excess money to meet future needs. Investing is not about trying to get rich quick. It is about making your money work for you and creating the means to support your family when you are retired.

Rules of Investing:

1) Never invest money you cannot afford to lose. All investments have an element of risk, and the possibility exists that you might lose all or a portion of the money you have invested. One only has to look at the variability in the stock market to see that this is true.

2) Never get involved with things you do not understand. Do not try to buy individual stocks unless you know the company well and have confidence that it is well-run.

3) Demand sufficient information to evaluate the opportunity thoroughly. Take the time to research possible investments thoroughly.

4) Seek good, non-involved Christian counsel. Many knowledgeable Christian financial counselors will discuss your needs and goals and help you make wise investment decisions.

   Proverbs 19:20 *"Listen to counsel and receive instruction, that you may be wise in your latter days."*

5) Set a minimum time to pray and seek God's direction. Don't let anyone rush you into an investment decision. If the opportunity is only available for a limited time, it is probably an opportunity you should forgo.

6) Once you have God's direction, write out an investment plan. A written plan will help you keep your goals in mind and help you make investment decisions consistent with your goals.

   Proverbs 20:5 *"Counsel in the heart of a man is like deep water, but a man of understanding will draw it out."*

7) Avoid "get rich" schemes. Plan for a slow, steady growth. If it sounds too good to be true, then it almost always is.

   Proverbs 21:5 *"The plans of the diligent lead surely to plenty, but those of everyone who is hasty surely to poverty."*

   Proverbs 28:20 – 22 *"A faithful man will abound with blessing, but he who hastens to be rich will not go unpunished. To show partiality is not good, because for a piece of bread a man will transgress. A man with an evil eye hastens after riches, and does not consider that poverty will come upon him."*

CONCLUSION

Cultivating True Wealth

In this final lesson, we look at true wealth and how to cultivate it. Money is a necessity in our world, and it serves many purposes. However, money in and of itself cannot bring true happiness, contentment, or joy. And money most certainly cannot buy eternal life.

The Bible teaches us that real wealth can only come from having a personal relationship with Jesus Christ. To enter into a personal relationship with Jesus, we must admit that we are sinners in need of a Savior, recognize that Jesus is the only one who can be our Savior, and accept His freely-offered sacrificial death as cleansing for our sins. Repentance and faith in Jesus lead to real peace on Earth and ultimately to an eternity in Heaven.

In Proverbs 22:4, King Solomon wrote that *"By humility and the fear of the Lord are riches and honor and life."* We must come to the Lord humbly admitting that we are sinners and in fear that He will give us the just punishment our sins demand before we can truly accept His gift of salvation. In accepting Jesus as our Savior, we become children of God and joint-heirs with Christ in the abundance of Heaven.

When the rich young ruler came to Jesus and asked what he must do to obtain eternal life, Jesus told him to obey the commandments. When pressed for what else was necessary, *"Jesus said to him, 'If you want to be perfect, go, sell what you have and give to the poor, and you will have treasure in heaven; and come, follow Me.'"* (Matthew 19:21) The next verse tells us, *"But when the young man heard that saying, he went away sorrowful, for he had great possessions."* (Matthew 19:22) This young man was so tied to his earthly riches that he was unwilling to give them up for the true riches of Heaven. How very sad! Our worldly possessions are fleeting, but real wealth will last forever.

Jesus further illustrated to His disciples the way to acquire real wealth by telling them the parable of the sheep and the goats, found in Matthew 25:31 – 46:

> *"When the Son of Man comes in His glory, and all the holy angels with Him, then He will sit on the throne of His glory. All the nations will be gathered before Him, and He will separate them one from another, as a shepherd divides his sheep from the goats. And He will set the sheep on His right hand, but the goats on the left. Then the King will say to those on His right hand, 'Come, you blessed of My Father, inherit the kingdom prepared for you from the foundation of the world: for I was hungry and you gave Me food; I was thirsty and you gave Me drink; I was a stranger and you took Me in; I was naked and you clothed Me; I was sick and you visited Me; I was in prison and you came to Me.'*

> *"Then the righteous will answer Him, saying, 'Lord, when did we see You hungry and feed You, or thirsty and give You drink? When did we see You a stranger and take You in, or naked and clothe You? Or when did we see You sick, or in prison, and come to You?' And the King will answer and say to them, 'Assuredly, I say to you, inasmuch as you did it to one of the least of these My brethren, you did it to Me.'*

> *"Then He will also say to those on the left hand, 'Depart from Me, you cursed, into the everlasting fire prepared for the devil and his angels: for I was hungry and you gave Me no food; I was thirsty and you gave Me no drink; I was a stranger and you did not take Me in, naked and you did not clothe Me, sick and in prison and you did not visit Me.'*

"Then they also will answer Him, saying, 'Lord, when did we see You hungry or thirsty or a stranger or naked or sick or in prison, and did not minister to You?' Then He will answer them, saying, 'Assuredly, I say to you, inasmuch as you did not do it to one of the least of these, you did not do it to Me.' And these will go away into everlasting punishment, but the righteous into eternal life."

As you read this, I urge you to consider whether you are cultivating real wealth through your relationship with Jesus Christ and your actions. If you are not, it's not too late to start. For those of you who know Jesus Christ as your Savior, I urge you to use the money wisely that God entrusts to you and honor God in all that you do.

APPENDIX A

Practical Tips for Money-Management

These tips for money management and ideas for saving money have been selected from books, magazine articles, and internet sites, including Crown Financial Ministries (crown.org) and Christian Financial Concepts (christianfinancialconcepts.com).

Tracking Expenses:

One of the most important tools in managing one's money is to track monthly expenses. In the past, this was generally accomplished by keeping a small notebook handy to write all expenses in, recording expenses on an Excel spreadsheet, or using the "envelope" system. The envelope system involves dividing one's paycheck into envelopes, each for a designated purpose; when the envelope is empty, no more money can be spent on that category of expenses until the following month.

In today's digital world, tracking expenses can be accomplished more easily by downloading an app onto one's phone, iPad, Kindle, or other electronic devices. Since we tend to have our devices with us at all times, it is a handy, easy way to track expenses. Regardless of the method you use, it is crucial to consistently track expenses for at least several months to identify where you are spending your money.

Expense Tracking Methods:

1) Small notebook in purse, pocket, or car
2) Cash envelopes
3) Phone app
4) Excel spreadsheet

Resources to Help Manage Finances and Honor God:

1) Crown Financial Ministries   crown.org
2) Christian Financial Concepts   Christianfinancialconcepts.com
3) Managing God's Money   managinggodsmoney.com
4) Ready for Zero   readyforzero.com/resources

Money-Saving Tips:

Most of us have some true-and-tried methods of saving money on the things we buy most often. However, we can always learn some new tricks. The tips below are categories by type of purchase to make it easier for you to find the tips.

Groceries:

1) Check grocery ads before planning your weekly meals. Shop advertised specials, especially for nonperishables.
2) Always use a written list and stick to it. Plan meals for the week before shopping.
3) Avoid taking your children grocery shopping.
4) Never shop for groceries while hungry.
5) Shop in bulk if it makes sense for your family.
6) Calculate the price per unit. Don't automatically assume that the larger size is more economical.
7) Try store brand products. These usually are cheaper than name brands and offer the same quality.
8) Use a calculator to total purchases. You can download a free calculator app onto your phone, so you always have a calculator handy.

9) Reduce or eliminate paper products.
10) Avoid processed and sugar-coated cereals. They are expensive, and many have little nutritional value.
11) Avoid prepared foods, such as frozen dinners, pot pies, and cakes. You can save money by doing more food prep yourself.
12) Determine good meat cuts that are available from roasts or shoulders, and have the butcher cut these for you.
13) Use manufacturers' coupons and rebates only if you were going to buy the items anyway. Double-check to make sure they are the best buy.
14) Do not buy from convenience stores except in case of an emergency.
15) Avoid buying non-grocery items in a grocery supermarket except when on sale. These usually are "high mark-up" items.
16) Make your own baby food by processing regular food in a blender.
17) Check every item as it is being scanned at the store and again when you get home.
18) Consider canning fresh vegetables whenever possible. Make bulk purchases with other families at farmers' markets and such. (NOTE: Secure canning supplies during off-seasons.)
19) Plant a small garden and grow your own fresh vegetables.

Dining Out:

1) Make eating out a special occasion.
2) Know where kids eat free and take advantage when eating out.
3) Order lunch size meals OR order dinner size meals and take leftovers home.
4) Search for coupons and specials online and in the newspaper.
5) Sign up for customer loyalty programs at your favorite restaurants.
6) Avoid buying desserts at restaurants.
7) Skip the ice cream shop and buy ice cream in the grocery store.
8) Rather than eating out, throw a potluck party with family or friends.
9) Make coffee at home; invest in an inexpensive pot for the office.
10) Bring your own snacks to work and take snacks in the car when running errands.
11) Pack lunches for work.

Vacations and Recreation:

1) Consider taking a stay-cation. Take days trips, go on picnics, visit museums and local places of interest.
2) Consider a camping vacation to avoid motel and food expenses. If you have not camped before, borrow camping equipment or rent an RV, rather than investing a lot of money into owning the items.
3) Rent DVDs instead of going to the movies. There are many options, such as RedBox and NetFlix. Watching movies at home also saves on popcorn and soda.
4) Have family game nights.
5) To reduce expenses and increase fellowship, consider taking vacation trips with two or more families.
6) If flying, use the least expensive coach fare. Early morning and red-eye flights can be significantly cheaper than flying at other times of the day. Book early and search for the best deals.
7) Check out books and movies from the library.

Clothing:

1) If you can sew, consider making clothes.
2) Make a written list of clothing needs and purchase during the "off" season when possible.
3) Select outfits that can be mixed and used in multiple combinations rather than as a single set.
4) Search discount outlets that carry unmarked name-brand goods.
5) Shop at authentic factory outlet stores for close-out values of top quality.
6) Select clothing made of home washable fabrics.
7) Use coin-operated dry-cleaning machines instead of commercial cleaners.
8) Repair damaged clothing as soon as possible to prevent damage from getting worse.
9) Learn to utilize all clothing fully (especially children's wear).
10) Check out Goodwill and the Salvation Army for clothing.

11) Have clothes swapping parties. Works for kids' clothes and adult clothes.
12) Use coupons and shop sales. Be careful, however, to buy only clothing that you actually need.

Medical Expenses:

1) Prevention is cheaper than treatment. Take good care of your body and eat healthy meals.
2) Teach children to eat the right foods and clean their teeth properly. A good diet, rest, and exercise will most likely result in better health.
3) Ask doctors and dentists in advance about costs.
4) Shop for prescriptions and use generic drugs when possible.

Gift-Giving:

1) Shop ahead for birthdays and anniversaries. Look for sales and use coupons.
2) Make gifts. Learn new skills, such as sewing and knitting.
3) If your family is large, draw names. Or only buy Christmas gifts for young children and immediate family members.
4) Help children earn money to shop for gifts.
5) Consider sending cards rather than gifts.

General:

1) Don't buy bottled water or $3 cups of coffee.
2) Have 'planned' leftovers for lunches and dinners on busy nights.
3) Look for things you need on Craigslist or eBay.
4) Take unwanted items to consignment stores.
5) Use your curtains and/or blinds to hold in heat in the winter and keep out heat in the summer.
6) Dishwashers save more water than hand washing dishes.
7) Wash clothes in cool or cold water. Most detergents work just as well in cold water.
8) Hang clothes out to dry.
9) Cut out or reduce cable expenses.

10) Reduce cell phone expenses. Consider eliminating your landline.

11) Eliminate magazine subscriptions and look for articles online.

12) Take reusable bags when you go shopping.

13) Reduce, reuse, and recycle.

14) Frame your own photos and artwork to hang on the wall.

15) When ordering online, look for free shipping.

16) Don't spend change. Put it in a jar and cash it in at the end of the year.

17) Put half of any money received for birthdays and bonuses in savings.

APPENDIX B

Basics of Salvation

The Bible teaches us that we are all sinners in need of salvation. Most people know that even without reading the Bible. You have probably been aware of your shortcomings since you were a very young child. You may admit that you need to be "saved" yet have no idea how to be saved or what salvation actually means. Or you may believe that if you are basically a good person, God will let you into Heaven when you die.

The Bible teaches us that we cannot be good enough to get to Heaven. Even one sin is too many. On our own, we are lost and hopeless. But, we have not been left on our own. God demands that a price be paid for sin, and He knew we could never pay that price. So, He sent His son, Jesus, to Earth to pay the price for us. Jesus led a sinless life. Yet, He was crucified on a wooden cross. The shedding of His blood paid the price for the sins of each person who has ever lived or who will live.

Salvation is a gift God offers to us. Like any gift, it does not become yours until you accept it. Jesus is offering this gift to you today. Will you receive it?

Accepting the free gift of salvation is as easy as ABC.

A: **Admit that you are a sinner.** *"For all have sinned and fall short of the glory of God."* Romans 3:23

B: **Believe that Jesus paid the price for your sins.** *"Believe on the Lord Jesus Christ, and you will be saved, you and your household."* Acts 16:31

C: **Confess your sins:** *"If we confess our sins, He is faithful and just to forgive us our sins and to cleanse us from all unrighteousness."* 1 John 1:9

If you are ready to accept this free gift that God is offering you, then pray this simple prayer:

Dear Lord,

I confess that I am a sinner and need Your forgiveness. I believe Your son Jesus died on the cross to save me from the just punishment of my sins. I ask You to come into my heart and forgive my sins. Thank You for saving me from my sins. Thank You for loving me. From now on, I will live for You. I ask You to be the Lord of my life. Please guide me and direct my path that I may walk every day with You, Lord. In the precious name of Jesus, Amen.

Printed in the United States
By Bookmasters